The Generous Husband

~ A Year of Generous Tips ~

TO MY
FAVORITE MUFFIN

FROM THE
GENEROUS HUSBAND

The Generous Husband

~ A Year of Generous Tips ~

PAUL H. BYERLY
Co-Creator of The Marriage Bed

THE GENEROUS HUSBAND
A Year of Generous Tips

Cover art by: Lori Byerly

First printing 2004

Published in Austin, Texas, by Karis Publishing, Inc.

Karis Publishing, Inc.
1019 Meredith Drive
Austin, TX 78748 USA

ISBN: 0-9718040-5-2

Printed and bound in the United States of America

This book is dedicated to:

The Lady on My Left

the wonderful lady who made me a
better man, and taught me what it
means to be truly generous.

Acknowledgements:

Naming a few risks leaving someone out, but there are several individuals who need to be mentioned: Jason and Alise, my underpaid (unpaid) proofreaders; the folks from church at Kurtis and Lisa's house who encouraged, prayed, and did not show any hint of being tired of hearing about this project; three generations of Dales for their friendship, encouragement, prayers, and help; The Marriage Bed prayer warriors, who have prayed for this book for more than a year; and the wonderful OG (the members of The Marriage Bed oversight group). Finally my thanks to my Lord Jesus Christ, without whom I could not have become generous.

Table of Contents

Forward	8
Introduction	9
How to Be a Generous Husband	10
A Year of Generous Tips	16
Special Occasion Tips	
Anniversary	29
	122
Her Birthday	91
Your Birthday	61
Child's Birthday	25
Buying Lingerie Without Dying of Embarrassment	184
Non-Sexual Massage	187
Cooking for Those "Clueless About the Citchen"	190
Extra Tips for Those Who Have Children at Home	198
The Flood, AKA Menstruation	204
Sexual Massage	208
Suggested Reading List	211
On-Line Resources	213

Forward

Almost twenty years ago, the Lord and a cherubic looking young man ganged up on me and helped me make the second best decision of my life. I married Paul. We had so many struggles, but he never gave up on me. He helped me face the demons of my past and later we walked out into the abundant life that you hear so much talk about. I couldn't be more blessed (well, maybe if I had more chocolate).

I don't know what I did to deserve the generous husband, but I'm grateful that God sent him my way. He makes me smile every day (and often laugh hysterically). He blesses me with his love, thoughtfulness, humor, and integrity. I hope you enjoy his writings as much I have enjoyed proofreading them. I encourage y'all to listen to the heart of what he shares. These principles put into action can transform your marriage and put a permanent smile on your wife's face. It is sincerely worth your time and effort.

Blessings, Lori <><

Introduction

How I Came to Write the Generous Husband

It's my wife's fault! I know men since Adam have said that, but I'm not putting blame on her, I'm giving her due credit.

About a decade ago, my wife Lori came to a conclusion based on her prayer time and in her Bible reading: those who follow Jesus should be very generous. Having decided this, she set out to do it, with our children and myself being her first victims. By the time she discussed it with me, I'd already seen the results of her efforts, and I was impressed. I was also challenged – a typical competitive male response, I suppose. I set out to be more generous to her than she was to me. I must confess, I have rarely succeeded at beating her, but I continue to try.

Next came the daily e-mail tips. Again, it's my wife's fault. We'd become increasingly involved in marriage ministry and had begun The Marriage Bed, an on-line ministry dealing primarily with sexuality. As we heard from (or read from) more and more couples, it became clear that many marriages suffered from a lack of generosity. Even when this is not the initial or primary problem, it works to make the situation worse. Thus the Generous Wife list was born. Once again, I was challenged to do likewise, and once again she surpassed me, with subscribers to her list almost double those to The Generous Husband.

With this as background, you will understand the pride I take in telling you that it was I, not my wife, who decided it was time to write the book I'd talked about doing for years. That part is my fault, and she copied me!

How to be a Generous Husband

Are you a generous husband? Never mind, your answer is not what counts; the real question is this: does your wife think you are a generous husband?

Generosity is one of those things in which perception is reality. If you give in ways she does not recognize, or fail to give what she really needs or where she really needs it, you have failed. It's like telling her you love her in Spanish when she speaks English and French – you may have done a fine job of expressing your love, but she is unaffected by the strange sounds you made.

This is the general premise of Gary Chapman's book *The Five Love Languages* – that each of us "hears" love in one of several ways. Chapman identifies these "love languages" as gifts, touch, acts of service, quality time, and words of affirmation. If your wife "hears" love in acts of service, but you're "speaking" love in gifts and touch, you will both become rather frustrated. She feels unloved, and you feel she can never be satisfied. (I strongly recommend the book *The Five Love Languages* – after the Bible it's probably the most marriage enriching and relationship-changing book you will ever read.)

Are you generous where she needs you to be?

We each have certain areas where we feel generosity strongly, and other areas where generosity affects us only a little or not at all. If you're failing to be generous to your wife in an area of deep need, she may not recognize your generosity in other areas. You need to know her deepest needs.

Where does she need you to be generous? Where does she feel empty, uncared-for, or neglected? Her past, and particularly her childhood, will have a great deal to do with her areas of greatest need. Ask her what she wanted and did not receive as a child, and what she feels her parents failed to do for her. Take those answers and project them onto her life now – what would be the corresponding adult needs and desires? If she felt it was unfair that she never had her own room as a child, perhaps she needs a "place of her own" now. If she never got a doll she wanted, look for things she would like to have now – even if they're not "practical." If she felt lonely, find ways to be in the same room she's in even when you are doing different things.

What makes her feel loved and appreciated?

Are there things your wife does that make you feel especially good? Do you feel particularly bad when she doesn't do these things? Your reactions to these things are probably exaggerated; you feel strongly blessed when she does them, and greatly denied when she does not. There are things that affect your wife in similar ways, and you need to learn what they are.

Think about the things that deeply affect you. Some of these things are simple, small, and seemingly insignificant. Some things may even seem a little silly – perhaps so silly you would hate to voice them. Again, your wife is the same way. Being aware of how sensitive you might be about such a discussion, ask your wife to tell you about the things you do or don't do that result in her feeling loved or unloved and appreciated or ignored. Don't argue or debate what she says, just listen. Don't make any promises other than to think and pray about what she shares. Do take what she says very seriously, and look for ways to make changes that will result in her feeling loved, appreciated, and generously blessed.

Go with who cares about it the most.

If you like to eat just about anything, and your wife is a fairly picky eater, does it not seem obvious that it's a good plan to let her choose which restaurant you go to? This same idea can be, and I think should be, applied to many areas of your marriage. Be quick to do it "her way" when you think she cares about something more strongly than you do.

Don't limit this to areas where you have no preference. If it matters a little to you, and a lot to her, then doing it her way is a good idea. If doing it your way inconveniences her or irritates her more than doing it her way would inconvenience or irritate you, do it her way. Even when both of you feel fairly strongly about something, if it's not absolutely huge to you, be generous and do it her way. Let your attitude be that you would rather be inconvenienced than have her be inconvenienced.

I'm not suggesting that you become a doormat, or give up all personal preferences. It's normal and healthy to have strong opinions about how certain things should be, or how they should be done. When something really matters to you, especially when it clearly matters more to you than it does to her, gently press for doing it your way. Note that one bonus of being generous about things she cares about is that she is far less likely to fight you on the things that are important to you.

Following the Example of Jesus

The Bible makes the analogy of Jesus' relationship with the Church being like that of husband and wife. I doubt any of us would call Jesus a wimp, but look at the things He "put up with" for us. Jesus, who was completely innocent, gave no defense of Himself before His crucifixion. At the last supper Jesus washed the disciples' feet – a task usually delegated to the lowest ranking servant; it would be like Jesus coming to your church and wanting to clean the toilets! Even on the cross, Jesus reached out in love to the thief on His right.

Consider some of the things that all believers are called to do: turn the other cheek, go the extra mile, if someone takes your coat give them your shirt too, loan without expecting to receive back, repay evil with good, bless those who curse you. If we are called to do these things for our neighbors, our acquaintances, and even our enemies, how much more should be we prepared to sacrifice and even to "be wronged" for the sake of our wife?

Is she just plain selfish?

Yes, there are women who are just plain selfish. Even women who consider themselves sincere, devoted Christians can be, or become, very selfish. I'll address that below, but first let me discuss a couple of situations where the husband might be able to do something to change his wife's selfishness.

I might talk to a man and have him tell me that he gives, and gives, and gives to his wife. He sacrifices for her, and does things that would cause most women to kiss his feet – and yet she's not happy, it's never enough, she always wants more, she's never satisfied. Then I talk to this man's wife, and I hear from her that he has never given her the one thing she wants and needs him to give. It could be respect, a house she can feel proud of (well kept, not beyond his means) or spending more time with their children. Whatever it is, it's not her latest "demand," it's the one thing she has asked for all along.

Perhaps her husband feels unable to give her what she needs, maybe he is unwilling to do what it would cost him to give it, or maybe it's his passive-aggressive way of hurting or controlling her. The reason he's not giving her what she needs is irrelevant to her, it's the lack that hurts her. No amount of giving in other areas, no matter how wonderful the giving is, will make up for denying her the one thing she most wants and needs.

Another possibility is that a selfish woman is trying to protect herself. She's been deeply hurt in the past – by her parents, by a former boyfriend or husband, or by someone else. She started to "look out for #1" because she felt that if she didn't, no one would. She bought into the world's mantra of protecting yourself, fighting only for yourself, doing unto others before they do unto you. If she has years of damage, or has been in "protection mode" for many years, a few months of generosity from her husband are not going to heal her wounds and cause her to suddenly become less selfish. But even in this situation a husband's generosity and unoffendable love can make a difference, if he keeps at it long enough. Give, and give, and keep giving. Don't expect a sudden massive change, but do look for little hints that your generosity is softening her heart. If you stay the course, you may reap a reward for both of you.

"If mama ain't happy, ain't nobody happy."

My wife, that generous lady, absolutely despises that saying – she is appalled that any woman would manipulate her family in that way. Yes, some women are just flat out selfish, with no underlying cause about which nothing can be done. I wish I had some way of changing such a woman, but I don't. As far as I can tell, God does not violate people's free will, no matter how hard we pray, or how righteous our prayers.

What is the proper, godly, response if your wife is a never satisfied, always wants more, never happy woman? It's easy to grow less and less generous, but is that right with God? In this situation, you must not allow your wife to affect or control you, and being less generous because of her actions would be putting her in control. Decide what is right, what would be proper for a woman who was reasonable, and give your wife that. Give freely and lovingly up to the line of what is right, then lovingly refuse to be manipulated, pressured, nagged, or bribed to do things that are not acceptable or reasonable.

If your wife is difficult and stubborn in any area, I highly recommend to you the book *Loving Solutions* by Gary Chapman. Even if the book does not result in change, it will help you to live in a difficult marriage without losing your mind.

A Year of Generous Tips

First, I should admit that some of these tips won't work for you. Because of what your wife likes and does not like, because of your marriage situation, because you do or do not have children, some of these tips will not fit. However, even when a tip does not fit your life, it can still teach you something about being generous. Think of these tips as both a fish a day and a how to fish guide – use them both to be generous and to learn how to be generous.

To the right of each date is a word or two indicating what the tip is designed to address. Five of these are based on the love languages Gary Chapman describes in his book *The Five Love Languages*. The categories are

Touch - The Physical Touch Love Language
Gifts - The Gifts Love Language
Service - The Acts of Service Love Language
Time - The Quality Time Love Language
Words - The Words of Affirmation Love Language
Communication - The Need for Good Communication
Prayer - The Need to Pray With and for Your Wife
Walk - The Need for a Shared Christian Walk
Sex - The Need for a Healthy Sex Life
Romance - The Need for Romance
Holiday - Holiday Ideas

January 01 Gifts/Holiday

A penny saved...

Get a large clear container and drop a penny into it. Tomorrow drop in 2 pennies. Each day increase the amount added by 1 cent, until you put in \$3.65 on December 31st. Designate the money for some special activity, something both of you want, or make it a gift for her to spend as she chooses.

Done as suggested above, this will put \$667.95 in the container in one year, so you may want to modify somewhat. Adding money every other day yields \$258.78 a year; every third day results in \$73.81 a year.

You can also add money daily for a set period of time, leading up to her birthday, your anniversary, or some other date. Daily for a month nets \$4.65. Two months is \$18.91, 3 months is \$41.86, 4 months is \$75.03, 5 months is \$117.81, and 6 months is \$168.36.

January 02 Prayer

Resolved...

I know, New Year's resolutions are a dime a dozen, but let me suggest one that you both can, and should keep. Resolve to be a better husband this year than you were last year. Whether you were an incredible husband or a horrible one last year, you know you could do better. Make a promise to yourself, and to the Lord, to do whatever needs to be done to be a more loving, giving, and generous husband.

January 03 Time

I have you scheduled for...

Buy a good size calendar or a desk date-book for your wife. Before giving it to her, write in what you are going to do with her on certain dates: movies, meals out, walks in the park, trips, and whatever else you can think of. Add new dates as the year progresses.

January 04 Time

Our Place

Find a restaurant or coffee shop to call "yours." Make it your special, private, place where the two of you go to spend time together.

January 05 Sex/Communication

Talking About Sex

How long has it been since you had a good open talk about sex? Have you ever had such a talk? Use the first of the year as an "excuse" to talk with your wife about your sex life. What do each of you enjoy? What would you each like more of, or like to change? What might you want to try that you've never tried before?

It's probably best to have this discussion sometime other than just before or after sex. If possible, pick a place other than the bedroom, and be sure you have plenty of time and privacy.

January 06 Service

Kids' Day Out

If you have young children, one of the best things you can do for your wife is give her some time at home without the children. Sunday is a great day to do this – take the family to lunch after church, then drop your wife at the house and take the kids out for the rest of day. Let her know that you will be back after dinner, and you and the kids will have already eaten. When you get home, be responsible for all that is involved in getting all the kids into bed.

➢➢ **She's worth it!** ⮜⮜
➢➢ **Three simple words,** ⮜⮜
➢➢ **One important truth:** ⮜⮜
➢➢ ⮜⮜
➢➢ **She's worth it!** ⮜⮜

January 07 Gifts

Don't Curse the Darkness

For most of us in the Northern Hemisphere, it's a cold, dreary time of the year, which makes scented candles a great gift. Candles add "warmth" to a room, and scented candles fill the room with a pleasing aroma. Look for scents like vanilla, cinnamon, bayberry, or spice.

January 08 Prayer

Praying by the Letters

Not sure how or what to pray for your wife? Do it by the first letter of the day of the week:

Sunday = Spiritual walk
Monday = Mood and emotions
Tuesday = Time and energy
Wednesday = Wellness – physical health
Thursday = Talents and gifts
Friday = Family and friends
Saturday = Sexuality

January 09 Words/Romance

Message in a Bottle

Find a fancy bottle with a cork (craft stores will have some). Write a love note, roll it up, and tie it with a ribbon. Drop the note in the bottle, cork it, and leave it where she will find it. Make sure she can get the note out without breaking the bottle; she's probably going to want to display the whole thing.

January 10 Touch

Stroke, stroke, stroke...

Brush her hair for her before she goes to bed. Hair brushing can be very relaxing, and it's a great way to help her unwind. You can talk with her, or be quiet; which ever you think will most bless her. Have her sit while stand or sit behind her (you can do this with both of you on the bed). If her hair is long, brush slowly from the top of the head to the ends. If her hair is short, use a brush with widely spaced, knobby "bristles" to give her a scalp massage. Occasionally touch her face and shoulders as you work.

January 11 Holiday /Gifts

Gifts with a Theme

Find some small thematic item to give each gift-giving holiday. For example, the M&Ms folks make little plastic M&M characters with holiday appropriate hats: a Santa hat, an Easter hat, etc. Refrigerator magnets are another good choice, as are small plaques or candle holders.

January 12 Sex/Service

A more flattering light…

Most women, even those who could be on the cover of a fashion magazine, worry about the way they look. This fear is especially strong when she's naked, and it can interfere with a woman's sexual freedom. One way to help lessen this concern is by providing soft lighting in the bedroom. Try one or more of the following:

- Get some coloured "party light bulbs" available at many stores, even at most grocery stores.
- GE makes a pink bulb that has a nice soft colour.
- Candles are always a good bet. Try a double or

triple wick candle for a reasonable amount of light, or put several votive candles around the room, especially in front of mirrors. (Be sure to put candles on something safe, watch for flammable things nearby, and put them out before you fall asleep.)

- If you know which end of a screw drive to use, install a dimmer switch for a bedside lamp. Home Depot® and other such places have dimmers that can easily be added to any lamp cord. Dimming a bulb not only provides softer light, it changes the colour of the light in an inviting way.

January 13 Time/Communication

The Talking Place

Create a special place dedicated to sitting together and sharing your thoughts and feelings. You could put a love seat in your bedroom, hang a porch swing, or put a couple of chairs under a tree in the back yard. Or, if you walk together regularly, find a bench, curb, or rock to sit on. Neither where you sit nor what you sit on matters, the point is to have a place reserved for the intimacy of communication.

Once you've decided where the place is to be, share with your wife that you want it to be a special place for talking. You may find she will sit there, or lead you there, to indicate a need to converse with you. Because our minds make connections between things and actions, and between places and feelings, you may also find that it becomes very easy for you to talk openly when you sit with your wife in your special place.

January 14 Gifts

A Very Small Rose Garden

Look for a miniature rose in a pot (this is the best time of year to get them). You may be able to find them at a grocery store or discount chain, or go to a garden center or nursery. Rose plants do well in a sunny window, and in many areas can be planted in the ground in the spring.

Brown thumb tips: Look for a plant with a lot of buds and very few open flowers – it may not be as impressive at first, but she will get to enjoy all the blooms. Check the tips of the smallest leaves – look for a plant without brown or wilted leaf tips. If the pot is in a plastic or foil sleeve, remove the sleeve or cut a hole in the bottom, so water can drain out. Place the pot on a plate or saucer. Wait until the surface of the soil is all but dry, and then give enough water to go through to the saucer.

January 15 Prayer

Informed Prayer

If you are regularly praying for your wife, does it matter if she knows about your prayers? Telling your wife you are praying for her won't make your prayers any better or more effective, but knowing you're praying for her will bless her. What will bless her even more is the knowledge that your prayers for/about her are guided, at least in part, by what's important to her. Ask her specifically what she would like you to be praying about for her. Listen to what she says and then repeat what you heard so you both know that you understand. End your talk with a quick prayer, and then continue taking your wife's concerns before the Lord in your private prayer time.

January 16 Touch

Fancy Foot Work

Anytime is a good time for a foot rub. Feet are often sore, and even if they're not, it just feels good to have them rubbed. If your wife tends towards ticklish, use a firm pressure and stay in contact with the skin rather than lifting your hands. A lotion is not essential since the skin on the feet is fairly tough, but it feels nice, can help reduce ticklishness, and can make her feet softer. Buy a fancy foot cream, or use any hand lotion or baby oil.

➢➢ *"Husbands, love your wives,* ➣➣
➢➢ *just as Christ also loved the church* ➣➣
➢➢ *and gave Himself for her,"* Eph 5:25 ➣➣

January 17 Words

Laying Your Card on the Table

Leave her a card telling her how wonderful she is. Mention something she's recently done which blessed or touched you, and thank her for being your wife.

January 18 Holiday

Of ponies and slumber parties...

If you have children, their birthdays are very special to your wife. Be a part of their birthdays – not just showing up for what she plans, be a part of the planning and preparing. Remember, when you bless your kids, you bless your wife.

January 19 Gifts/Sex

Give her a what??

Valentine's Day is less than a month away. If you want to try a sexual gift this year, check the On-line resources on page 213 for a clean, Christian, "sex stuff" site. You'll find mildly sexual items like lotions and massage oils, more sexual items like chocolate body paint, and items that are "more daring."

January 20 Service

Work from the top down.

To do acts of service right, you need to do the things she most wants/needs you to do. If you are faithfully doing numbers 4 through 100 on her priority list, but not doing numbers 1 through 3, she's going to feel frustrated, and maybe even, unloved. Do you know what's at the top of her list? Are you sure? Why not ask her? Better yet, get her to write it down.

January 21 Touch

A Touchy Little Game

Get a die, or a pair of dice, and write up a code sheet for what each number means. For example:

1 = a hug
2 = a kiss
3 = foot rub
4 = back massage
5 = face massage
6 = hand massage

Leave the dice and the code sheet by the bed, on an end table near the couch, or anywhere else that seems appropriate. Tell her she may roll the die and receive the indicated touch whenever she likes.

Tip: If you use a pair of dice, some numbers will come up more often than others. Assign the "expensive" touches to hard to roll numbers.:

2 will roll 1 way (3%)
3 will roll 2 ways (5.5%)
4 will roll 3 ways (8%)
5 will roll 4 ways (11%)
6 will roll 5 ways (14%)
7 will roll 6 ways (16.5%)
8 will roll 5 ways (14%)
9 will roll 4 ways (11%)
10 will roll 3 ways (8%)
11 will roll 2 ways (5.5%)
12 will roll 1 ways (3%)

January 22 Time

A picnic this time of year?

Time for a nice, quiet, late night picnic – in your house. Spread a blanket on the floor, add a couple of pillows, and set out whatever you and your wife like to snack on. Put on a CD with quiet music, or better yet some "outdoors sounds" like crickets, rain, or ocean waves. Turn out all the lights, and light a small votive candle. Relax, feed each other, talk, and hold each other.

Hint: If you can set this up without her catching you, it's a nice surprise to spring on her.

➢➢ **She's worth it!** ➢➢

January 23 Holiday/Gifts

Give her chocolate and no one will get hurt!

Valentine's candy is in the store, so it's time to buy chocolate! Get there while the getting is good. There are a few exceptions, but most women really, really enjoy chocolate. So, no matter what else you do for Valentine's Day, get her at least a bit of chocolate. Even if she's on a diet, give her at least a Hershey's kiss.

Tip: Chocolate roses make a nice gift – buy one or two and put them in a vase with some real roses.

January 24 Sex

Good Clean Sex

When was the last time you took a shower together? It's inherently sexual, and a great place for foreplay ... or more. Pick a time when she's not too tired, and keep an eye on her reactions as you go, especially if this is something new.

Start with a good washing. Have her face the spray of hot water while you stand behind her, and slowly wash her backside with far more lather than you need. Work from the top down, spending extra time on her back and buttocks. When you arrive at her feet have her turn around, and work up her front side. Note that soap and female genitals are not a good mix, so just "shampoo" her pubic hair as you go past. Wash her breasts extra well and very slowly. If you have a showerhead that comes of the wall, you can have fun rinsing her off. A spray of warm water on her vulva can be arousing (or even lead to orgasm if she is so inclined and willing to instruct you), but don't set it to hard pulsating spray! When she is rinsed off give her a long hug with her back to the warm water and her front to the warm you.

When you step out of the shower, grab a towel, and dry her off. Then, follow your instincts...

January 25 Communication

I didn't hear it from the grapevine.

When you have news, especially "big news," be sure your wife is the first person with whom you share the news. Doing this tells her that she is first in your book, and that you want to share things with her. Even with "small news," making sure she hears about it from you, rather than someone else, will make her feel loved and thought about.

January 26 Service

Be her man who wears the star.

Women still tend to be treated as second-class citizens by many car care places, so take care of the registration, inspection sticker, oil changes, and other regular car maintenance for all the cars.

January 27 Holiday/Romance

This one goes out to...

If your wife listens to a certain music radio station, try to dedicate a song to her on your anniversary. Even if the station doesn't usually do requests or dedications, you might be able to get them to do so for your anniversary if you inquire in advance. Be sure to choose a song in the station's regular rotation.

January 28 Prayer/Words

"... and the hands that prepared it."

When you bless your meals, take the opportunity to thank the Lord for your wife, and/or ask Him to bless her. Make a habit of blessing her each time you bless a meal. If she has a special need, make a short mention of that – just don't go so long the food gets cold!

Hint: Make a point of being grateful for your wife even when you say grace in a public setting.

January 29 Touch

Can you feel me now?

Strip down to your undies (bra and panties for her) and climb into bed to snuggle, touch, and kiss everywhere there's no cloth. Make it clear that this is not foreplay, but enjoyment of all the other wonderful kinds of touch you can give and receive.

While this is not intended to be sexual, it will almost certainly be very arousing for you, just set that aside and try to enjoy the non-sexual aspects. Be prepared to end without sex, but if it's also arousing for her, and she lets you know that, you can do whatever seems prudent at that point!

➢➢ *"An excellent wife is the* ⮘⮘
➢➢ *crown of her husband."* Pr 12:4a ⮘⮘

January 30 Time

Four Helping Hands

Volunteer to help others, as a couple. Do yard work for an older individual, help someone move, offer to watch someone's kids, or find a community service program you can do together.

January 31 Holiday

Valentine's – Celebrated

Ever notice how the birthdays of famous people are "moved" to Mondays so we can get a 3-day weekend? If Valentine's falls on a day that's just not convenient for you to do something you would like to do, such as take her out to eat, move your celebration to another day. Give her the card and the chocolate on the 14th, and let her know you want to extend the celebration to whatever day you will "wine and dine" her.

February 01 Sex

A story for an audience of one ...

Write a sexual story for your wife, a story that "stars" the two of you. Leaving a story like this for your wife to find can be a great form of pre-foreplay. Alternatively, read it aloud to her in bed.

Story telling is a safe way to explore things you've wondered about, but are unsure of, or things you're worried she might react to negatively. If you've wondered what it would be like to try a certain position, try it in a story. If she says, "I've thought about that," or "that might be fun," you can take it from there. A story can also be a good way to tell her what you feel and think about when you make love with her; use it as a window into the inner workings of the man she loves.

As you write, be aware that she's a woman, and as such does not think about sex the same way you do. Don't run her over with a lot of explicit language and nonstop “action.” Describe the setting, the colours, the smells, and the textures. Give the story some real emotional content, and don’t end it the moment the sex is over; write about the “after glow” too. If she enjoys your story, suggest she try her hand at writing one for you – who knows what you might learn!

February 02 Valentine’s Gifts

Shop Early

It’s time to do the Valentine’s shopping before everything is picked over. The best cards go fast, so start there. Gifts that go over well for most women are candles, stuffed animals, and anything with “romantic words.” Ideas suited to certain love languages follow.

➢➢ *“Drink, yes, drink deeply,* ⋞⋞
➢➢ *O beloved ones!”* SoS 5:1b ⋞⋞

February 03 Romance/Valentine’s Gifts

Love in Four-part Harmony

Local chapters of the Barbershop Harmony Society will send a quartet to deliver a card, sing a love song or two, and maybe give her a rose or candy. Prices range from to $35 to $50. Check your phone book, or try the on-line location service at www.singingvalentines.com.

Other singing ideas are a restaurant with a singer, or getting a few couples together and splitting the cost of a quartet with the other men.

February 04 Words/Valentine's Gifts

The Card Thing

Yes, I know Hallmark makes a bundle on Valentine's cards. But your wife will be blessed by it, so fork over the money. Be sure to write something more than you name before you seal it up – a few short lines expressing your love for her are a must.

February 05 Prayer/Communication

How do you pray for me?

Ask her what she prays when she prays for you. Don't correct her or challenge her, just listen. Her prayers for you are a window into how she sees you, how she feels about you, and her worries about you. If you don't like what her prayers say about you, maybe you need to do some praying.

➤➤ **She's worth it!** ≺≺

February 06 Sex/Valentine's Gifts

Chocolate and Lace

Give a Valentine's gift that's something for both of you – a box of sexy lingerie with a heavy sprinkling of chocolate. Shop now, as the best of both products will be disappearing shortly. For hints on how to buy lingerie, see the "Buying Lingerie Without Dying of Embarrassment" section on page 184.

February 07 Touch

Hands she will want all over her.

Her skin is softer and more delicate than yours, especially on those parts you most want to touch! If your nails are rough, or your skin is hard, your touch will be a mixed blessing. Keep those nails trimmed and even, and use a good hand lotion as often as needed.

My personal recommendation for lotion is Corn Huskers Lotion®. My work in landscape and irrigation has my hands in dirt, water, gas, oil, and a number of chemicals on a daily basis, but with regular use of Corn Huskers® my hands cause no discomfort when I touch that Generous Wife of mine.

February 08 Service/Valentine's Gifts

Service in an Envelope

Buy a box of kids' valentines, the kind we used in elementary school. Pick a dozen or so from the box, and write "good for one ______" – and fill the blank with some "act of service" that you can perform for her. Seal them up, write something sweet or silly on the outside of each, and give them to her or leave them where she will find them.

February 09 Gifts/Valentine's Gifts

Many Gifts

If gifts are her thing, quantity can be more fun than quality (quality being spelled $$$ here). Get a single flower, a single balloon, a few small boxes of candy, a pair of sexy undies, and several cards. Give the gifts to her throughout the day, or put them where she will find them one at a time.

February 10 Sex

More Fore

Because they are painfully aware that they are slower to "get going" sexually, many women feel they must "get to" intercourse before their husband becomes frustrated. This may be true of your wife even if you've never expressed any impatience, or tried to rush her in any way.

Try extending foreplay, and see what happens. Don't act on her first hint that she is "ready." If she says something, let her know you will move to intercourse if that's what she wants, but you would enjoy seeing what it would be like to slow things down a bit. Even if she's able to "make do" with shorter foreplay, she will probably enjoy taking more time. She may also enjoy intercourse more as a result of more foreplay, and slow, prolonged foreplay can result in much stronger climaxes for both of you.

February 11 Words

"Thank you."

"Thank you" – two simple words, a common, courteous phrase. How you say "thank you," as well as when you say it, can change it from a nicety to a deeply encouraging blessing. The next time she does something nice for you, take her hand, look into her eyes, and say, "Thank you."

February 12 Time/Valentine's Gifts

Clink

No matter what's going on in your life, carve out a bit of time to be alone with her on Valentine's Day. Have a bottle of wine (or sparkling grape juice, or whatever) ready. Pour a couple of glasses, and toast your relationship with something like "Here's to the best wife God created."

February 13 Service/Romance/Valentine's Gifts

Will she leave a tip?

Even if it's cereal with sliced fruit, having it brought to you in bed is special, especially on February 14th A rose bud (in a new vase), or a new coffee mug, makes for a nice touch.

Hot Tip: If you can get away with it, serve her wearing nothing more than a dress shirt and a tie!

February 14 Touch/Valentine's Gifts

Rub her the right way.

Give her a Valentine's rub down, anything from a simple back rub to a full body massage. Make it as sexual or non-sexual as you think she would enjoy, and be sure to tell her you love her as you massage.

February 15 Gifts

Half Price

If she's a gifts person, this is the time to stock up! The stores are eager to dump the left over Valentine's stuff so they can put out Easter things, and they will make it worth your while to help them out. Buy now, and give over the next few months. Don't forget the half price candy if she's a chocolate fanatic.

February 16 Sex

Wanted: More Kissing

Most male types have no idea how important kissing is to women. Kissing in general is appreciated, and kissing as a part of sex is vital. It's not just in her head, there's a good biological reason why women are so turned on by kissing. Pheromones, which I like to call "airborne hormones," affect an organ inside the nose. You don't smell pheromones, but inhaling them can have powerful affects on your body. Women are far more sensitive to, and more affected by, pheromones than men are. What does this have to do with kissing? Kissing just happens to be a great way to share a dose of your own personal pheromones; and when you do so it "gets her going"!

My suggestion is to spend more time kissing. Kiss her all day long, from little kisses to long passionate ones. Kiss her when you first start to make love to her, and keep kissing her as you move on to "more sexual" activities.

Hint: Don't forget to kiss her after sex.

February 17 Walk

Assemble and Stir

"And let us consider one another in order to stir up love and good works, not forsaking the assembling of ourselves together..." Hebrews 10:24-25a

We generally think of that Scripture as a warning not to miss church, but it's really much more. We need to have close, accountable relationships with other followers of Jesus in order fulfill that scripture. As a married couple, we need to share this kind of relationship with other couples. If you have these kinds of friends, be sure not to forsake assembling with them outside of church. If you don't have these kind of friends, start inviting "candidates" over for a meal.

February 18 Service

Don't tax your wife.

In the USofA April 15th is the dead line for filing federal income taxes. Many folks wait until the last minute to do their taxes, or to discover they can't do it in time and file an extension instead. Women are far more concerned about this kind of thing than we men are, and it can really eat at them. The last minute rush is a point of aggravation and stress for many couples, and even if your wife says nothing, chances are it bothers her if you wait until April to start working on the taxes.

If you've been guilty of waiting too long to get your taxes done, make a promise to yourself right now that this year they will be done by April 1st. If you're going to owe money, and want to wait to mail your return, finish it early and mail it on due day.

February 19 Time

Quantity vs. Quality

How much quantity of time does it take to have real quality time? Sure, you can have a quality minute, but if all your quality time is crammed into short bits of time, don't expect it to fill her need for time.

A part of her quality time need is feeling that she is important enough to deserve your time. Always cutting quality time as short as possible does **not** send that message. Just being together, even if you are really doing nothing, is what she wants. Walking hand in hand together, laying together, doing the bills together, washing the dishes together ... See the pattern? The together part is what's important!

February 20 Words/Sex

What a lover you are!

Many women, maybe most women, worry that they are not really satisfying their husband in bed. Some women become so convinced they could never be a good lover that they stop trying! Make a point of telling her when she does something sexual that you enjoy. If she pleases you most or all of the time, tell her so. If she isn't doing too well, look for something you can praise her for – it might get her interested in trying harder. Even a simple but heartfelt "WOW" after sex will help her feel like a good lover.

February 21 Touch

It's That Time!

Pick a time of the day when you are usually with your wife. Each day, at that time, stop whatever you are doing and give her a kiss. Don't tell her why, just let her figure it out.

Tip: Kiss her in public if "the time" comes while you're out.

February 22 Gifts

Fake ID

Make her a member of the "world's best wife club," or "association of moms beyond measure," or "women of worth," or even the "great in bed club." Get a "mug shot" picture, print out a card, glue them together, and get it laminated. On the back of the card put "this card entitles the person shown on the front to ...." and fill in "kisses on demand" or whatever else sounds right.

February 23 Communication

Pink is a colour (salmon is a fish & peach is a fruit).

Compared to you, more of your wife's brain is devoted to language. That's why she tends to talk more, and to put so much more detail in what she says. As Ed Cole explains it, men want, and give, headlines, while women want, and give, the full story.

You can't change how God made her brain, nor

can you change your brain, but if you understand the difference, you can make some accommodations that will facilitate communicating with your bride. Lovingly "put up with" what you see as her verbal excess, and listen well enough to extract the headline from what she says; when you're the one talking, try to give her a bit more than just the headlines.

➢➢ *"the glory of children is their father."* ⮘⮘
➢➢ Pr 17:6b ⮘⮘

February 24 Sex

Move up a couple of inches.

"Let her breasts satisfy you at all times; And always be enraptured with her love." Pr 5:19b

I know you enjoy touching your wife's breasts, but does she enjoy it as much as she could? The upper portion of the breast, from 10 o'clock to 2 o'clock, is very pleasure sensitive; in some women touch here is more arousing that simulation of the nipples. Try stimulating the entire breast with the palm or heel of the hand.

Bonus: Breast sensitivity changes as a woman become aroused. As she approaches climax she may enjoy stronger stimulation than she would want at other times.

February 25 Service

Use Me!

Schedule a couple of hours to be available for whatever she needs you to do. Be sure to give her that time with a willing heart. Remember, when you're asked to go one mile, go two!

February 26 Time

Dream together, do together.

Work together to plan, and then do some home or yard improvement project. It could be anything from a small flowerbed to a total redo of the landscape, or a bit of interior touch up to a major remodeling job. Be sure to really listen to her thoughts, both as you plan and as you do the job.

February 27 Touch

Stand up for massage!

Give your wife a standing massage. This is a dry, fairly fast massage, and it's really about touch, not a true massage. Have her stand in the center of the room, preferably nude, feet barely apart and eyes closed. Massage her from the feet to the head, moving each stroke upward, and moving in a circle around her as you go. Lift her arms slightly to work on them. Finish with her face, and then give her a long hug and a kiss.

February 28 Gifts

Dying vegetation means I love you!

Giving flowers may seem unimaginative, but there's a good reason why flowers are a time honored gift for women – women like them! Of course, you can make it even better by getting just a bit fancy:

- Buy a small vase and keep a fresh flower in it all the time. Vary the flower type and colour. You should be able to get away with changing the flower 2 or 3 times a week.
- Build a bouquet one flower at time. You can do this over one day, or several. Buy the flowers all at once, or a few at a time, and stash them away in a cool place in a holding vase. Slowly slip the flowers in one at a time, so there are more there each time she sees it.
- Place an empty vase in a prominent place. Buy a full bouquet and parcel it out around the house, letting her find each flower and build the bouquet as she does.

Brown Thumb Tips: Buy flowers that are not yet fully open, they will last longer. When you get the flowers home put warm (not hot) water in the vase, cut off at least half an inch from the bottom of the stem with a diagonal cut, and put it immediately into the warm water. If the store has some of those little foil packs of preservative get some, it really does help.

Note: If this is not a leap year, do the next tip today as well. Double up, **she's worth it!**

February 29 Words

Encourage. Repeat.

It takes something like a dozen positive statements to balance or counteract one negative statement. If your wife was picked on growing up, or if her family put her down, she has a large backlog of negative comments that need to be counteracted. Regularly tell her that she is smart, or clever, or pretty, or a great cook, or a good mother, or...

March 01 Communication

The eyes have it.

Communication is far more than just the words we use. Our body language, our tone of voice, and how we look at someone, all send a great deal of information that can modify how our words are heard, or drown out our words. Be aware of these things, and how they add to or detract from your communication with your bride.

Bonus: The eyes can communicate more love and caring than our words can. When you really want her to know you love her, appreciate her, need her, or can't live without her, look her in the eyes as you tell her.

March 02 Sex/Touch

Foreplay Overload

Gather various items to touch/rub all over her body. Some good items are feathers, a soft paintbrush, a piece of fur or velvet, and a silk scarf.

Have her get naked and lay face down on the bed. Use each item in turn, slowly touching her entire backside with each. Be careful not to tickle. When you're done with her back, have her roll over and do the same on her front side. Pay extra attention to her face and breasts, but give her genitals only a brief, playful touch. By the time you're finished she may already be highly aroused, and it's time to zero in on her sex organs. Part her legs a bit more, if needed, and pick an item to use. Stimulate her with only the item: first around the genitals, the labia, and then focus on the clitoris. Add a bit of lubricant to make it even nicer (whatever you use if you have some – baby oil is good if you don't use condoms or a diaphragm). If it seems she could orgasm from what you're doing, and you don't think she would mind doing so, go for it. Otherwise move to intercourse shortly before she loses her mind.

Tip: If she's okay with it, the experience will be more powerful if she is blindfolded. Alternately, use very low light, such as a candle.

March 03 Service

[Bump] "Ouch!"

Is there some place in your house that is too dark? It could be a hallway, a bathroom, or maybe a closet? Make life a little easier, and a bit safer, by installing a "dusk to dawn" night light or a battery operated self-stick light.

March 04 Prayer/Walk

Pray about it later.

The next time your wife voices or shows frustration with something you've said or done, make a mental note of the incident. Later, take some time to pray and meditate about the situation. Is there some way of modifying your behaviour that would reduce her frustration? Were you abrupt, condescending, distant, or sarcastic? Even if you're sure it's her, not you, there's very likely something you could do to make it easier for both of you.

➢➢ *"A man shall leave his father and mother* ⮘⮘
➢➢ *and be joined to his wife, and the two* ⮘⮘
➢➢ *shall become one flesh."* Mt 19:5b ⮘⮘

March 05 Gifts

Ready Gift Reserve

If gifts are what speak to your wife, be ready at all times. First, you will need a good place to hide gifts until you give them to her; a box in the middle of a stack of boxes is a good place – she probably doesn't check old tax records regularly! Next, you need to learn to keep an eye out for things you know she would like. Buy several of something when you see them, and give them over time, separated by other gifts.

The woman who "hears" love in gifts is usually more moved by the thought than the price. A big expensive gift is always appreciated, but several small inexpensive gifts will have a greater affect on her. Similarly, regularly given “small” gifts are more valued than a rarely given “big” gift.

March 06 Touch

Knees kneed love too.

Do you pay much attention to her knees and elbows? Spend some time rubbing, stroking, massaging, and kissing them.

March 07 Time

Veg out together.

Gardening as a couple is a good way to spend time together. Even in an apartment, you can do container gardening if you have a porch or a sunny window. Get some pots and grow tomatoes and peppers. If space is does not allow even this, buy some 4 inch pots, grow some herbs on a windowsill.

March 08 Service

Got milk? Need eggs? How ‘bout...

When she runs out of something that she needs right now, be quick to say, “I’ll go get it.” Even if she was not hinting, nor expecting you to do it, go for whatever she needs.

Bonus: Bring back a cute card, a flower, or some chocolate.

March 09 Words

Good Morning!

The first voice your wife hears in the morning may well be yours, and the first words she hears from you can set the tone for her entire day. Be sure your morning greeting is one of love and encouragement.

March 10 Sex

I'm behind you all the way, babe.

Rear entry intercourse is the third most popular position, according those who count such things. However, doing it in a way that is comfortable for her can be a bit tricky. The problem is getting your bodies at the right relative height so you are not creating too much pressure and friction on one part of the vaginal entrance. Try the ideas below to alter how you fit together:

- She can change the angle and position of her vagina by how far she bends at the waist.
- Being on all fours will probably be more difficult for her than being on her knees and lowering her head and shoulders to the bed.
- If you're both standing, she can lean over and put her hands on a chair or the bed.
- If you are too tall, a pair of high heels can help, or you can vary your relative height by having your legs between hers (makes you higher) or having your legs outside hers (makes you lower).

Make adjustments until she finds what feels best for her.

March 11 Gifts/Romance

Write on, wife.

Find a specialty pen company and get some pens made that say something like “Your husband loves you,” “this pen belongs to a beautiful woman,” or “Lori B – World’s Best Wife” (putting in her name might bless her even more).

Hint: Try searching for sources by putting “imprinted pens” (with the quotes) in a web search engine. You can also get pens done at some copy shops.

March 12 Touch

Touch me ... NOW!!

Find something your wife can wear to indicate she’s touch hungry. Let her know that when she puts on whatever you choose (buy something new) you will see it as a signal to hug, hold hands and kiss more. The signal item can be anything: a certain shirt, a piece of jewelry, perfume, a hair clasp, a scarf, whatever.

Hint: Pick something you like, because you may be seeing it often!

March 13 Time

Fair Game

A good way to spend time together is to find a game you both enjoy. It’s more than just the game, because you’ll be focusing on her, giving her your time, and talking with her as you play. You want a game that is not too complicated (it's hard to talk over a chess game). You don't want one person to lose all the time, so pick something at which you are more or less equally matched, which allows you to handicap, or is mostly chance. Some good couple's games are Scrabble, Backgammon, card games, and dominos.

Hot Bonus: Make the game more interesting with one extra rule – the loser of each round has to remove a piece of clothing. Play until one of you is naked. Beware; she is less visually aroused, so her lack of covering is more of a handicap for you than yours is for her!

March 14 Service

The Money Talk

Do you think taking care of finances without letting your wife know what's going on "takes the pressure off of her," so she won't worry about money? In reality, it may have the opposite effect. When things are good she may worry needlessly, and when she knows money is tight she may fear something much worse than the truth.

What if you were suddenly unable to take care of the finances? Would she know how to step in and take care of it? Take some time to inform your wife about the finances. Tell her how things are, what the future looks like, and what the short and long-term plans are. Give her a cheat sheet; a detailed rundown of what money you have, what accounts and bills you have, the dates recurring payments are due, and where important documents are kept.

Even if your wife is involved in your finances, make sure she could easily find everything if she needed to. Don't forget to up-date her cheat sheet as needed.

March 15 — Walk

Make a Joyful NOISE!

Sing, whistle, or hum hymns, praise songs, or modern Christian music together. Remember, no matter how it sounds to you, God likes it!

March 16 — Sex

Leave it on.

Nudity is great, especially for sex, but for variety try seeing how much clothing you can leave on and still "complete the act." Have foreplay without removing anything, then move or take off only as much as necessary to have intercourse.

Aside from being fun, this "exercise" forces you to think a bit differently. Your usual sex routine won't work, so you won't be able to just default to autopilot. If you pay attention, you could learn things worth knowing.

Bonus: Try to give her an orgasm while she's fully dressed, without moving or reaching under any clothing. If you really understand her body, it's not that difficult, and if you don't understand her body, trying to do this could teach you something important!

March 17 Holiday/Touch

Is she greenless?

It's St. Patrick's Day. If you catch her not wearing green, I suggest kissing over pinching. Maybe some other "punishment" could be used in the bedroom!

March 18 Time/Communication

Spring, Summer, Winter, and Fall

The first day of spring is March 20th (sometimes March 21st depending on the year). Find a nice park or public garden, and take your wife there every couple of months to watch the seasons change. Use this as an opportunity to talk about the changes in your lives and in your marriage, and to make plans for the future.

March 19 Gifts

Gift Baskets

Gift baskets are very big now, so jump on the bandwagon. If you do it yourself, it won't cost a fortune, and you can tailor it to your wife. Go to a craft store and get a real basket, or find something else "basket like" – a box, a serving bowl, or a fancy plant pot. Line with tissue paper and fill with whatever. Make a bath basket with soap, bath oils and the like, or make an all chocolate bowl, or do her favourite foods, or books, or a movie basket (include some microwave popcorn). Arrange the items so all can be seen, then cover the basket with coloured cellophane (craft store again) or coloured plastic food wrap (grocery store). Finish it off with a bow and a card.

March 20 Words/Romance

High Tech Love Notes

If your wife has a pager, or a phone that accepts digital messages, you can send love notes that will mean nothing to anyone else, even if they see them. Just work up a short list of codes, and you're all set. For example:

111 = you're my number one lady
143 = I love you
34 = a hug and a kiss
777 = you are such a Godly wife
911 = need you right now!
411 = thinking of you
123 =you can count on me

March 21 Holiday/Service

There's something on your collar.

Easter dates: 3/27/05, 4/16/06, 4/8/07, 3/23/08, 4/12/09, 4/4/10, 4/24/11, 4/8/12, 3/31/13, 4/20/14, 4/5/15

If you're going to get your wife a corsage for Easter Sunday (hint, hint), get it by the Friday before Easter (store in the refrigerator – it will be fine). You may be able to pick up a very nice corsage at a large grocery chain, or go all out and hit a florist for an extra special one.

Hint: If you have a daughter (or more than one), consider buying for all the ladies in the house.

March 22 Sex

Good Clean Sex

Women's sense of smell is better than men's. This means body odor and bad breath turn them off a lot faster, and lot more strongly than the same things affect us. If you want your wife to enjoy you being intimately close, be sure you have taken care of all the necessary clean up.

March 23 Time

Green Light for Time Together

You can do some great talking in the car. It's private, and aside from all the folks out there who don't know how to drive, there are no distractions. The next time one of you needs to run an errand that involves the car, why don't you go together?

March 24 Service

Yes, I do windows.

Clean the windows for her. Inside, any window cleaner product and newspaper works well. On the outside easily reached windows can be done the same way, or use a squeegee to get it done faster. For high or otherwise difficult to reach windows, try one of the attach-to-the-garden-hose spray-on products.

➢➢ *"Let your fountain be blessed,* ➣➣
➢➢ *And rejoice with the wife of your youth."* ➣➣
➢➢ Pr 5:18 ➣➣

March 25 Communication

We need to talk.

None of us likes to have an argument or disagreement, but avoiding issues is even harder on your marriage in the long run. Even if the issue seems to go away "on its own," the underlying problem is still there. Over time, things that have been ignored can pile up and cause a lot of pain and damage.

If you're the one who keeps things from being talked out, you have the power to change that. If she's the one who avoids talking about problem, you will have to work a bit harder. If you can't do it alone, get some help from a pastor, a lay counselor, or a professional counselor.

Tips: Don't talk things out when either of you is tired, stressed, or has had a bad day. Make sure you have the time and privacy to work through things. Don't run her over; crushing her into agreeing or causing her to withdraw solves nothing. When she is talking, listen rather than planning your rebuttal. If you seem stuck, agree to think about it separately and talk again later. Finally don't think you have to agree 100%; if you can find a solution you can both live with that's enough.

March 26 Walk

Give time together.

The Lord wants more than just our money; He wants our time too. Find something you and your wife can do together to give of your time to your church, some other ministry, or an outreach to the poor, widows, or children.

You don't have to have great skills or do something major to make a difference; something as simple as weekly cleaning a building or mowing a lawn will save an organization the cost of hiring someone to do the work. Helping a single mother or widow repair something at her house will cost you far less than what it would cost her to get the work done. Volunteering for a non-profit organization allows you to do good things that might otherwise not be done.

"God can't cash out of state checks in Heaven. He needs you!" Keith Green in *Open Your Eyes*

March 27 Service

A Timely Blessing

Doing things for your wife, even little things, is a great way to bless her – but for maximum affect, timing is everything. When she's tired, getting up to fill her glass, or bringing her something she needs, will mean a great deal to her. Tucking the kids in when she's had a long day means a lot more than doing the same thing when she has not had a long day. Rubbing her feet when she's been on them all day is "worth more" than doing the same when her feet don't hurt.

The ultimate blessing comes from being the one to jump at doing things when you're both tired. From "I'll take care of dinner" to "I'll go out and get the mail," you can show your love by doing little things she would do, before she gets up to do them.

March 28 Time

Dinner for Two

If your wife values time spent with you above all else, dinner out is more about having you to herself than the food or the ambiance of the restaurant. Keep this in mind, and plan dinner for just the two of you at least once a month.

Tips: If funds are tight, take her to Taco Bell®. If you can't leave the kids, have a fancy dessert by candlelight after they are in bed.

March 29 Sex

Sex as a Part of the Whole Relationship

In one Corinthians seven, the Apostle Paul tells us that we are responsible for sexually satisfying our wife. What Paul does not say is that it's impossible to do this if we do not first properly satisfy our wife's need for intimacy and closeness. Men have the unfortunate ability to separate their penis from their heart and mind, allowing them to have sex without love or relationship. Because we are men, we are usually able to continue being sexual with our wife even when our emotional relationship is not what it should be; but most women do not have the ability to disconnect their sex organs from their hearts and minds. When a woman is not feeling close and intimate to her husband, it significantly reduces her ability to want, much less enjoy, sex. Your wife may be so sensitive to relationship issues that her sexuality can suffer a great deal before you're even aware there's any emotional distance or lack.

If you want your sex life to be better, look first and foremost at the non-sexual parts of your marriage. Are there places you're failing to love your wife? Does she feel your love? Do you give her the time she needs to feel close and intimate with you? Have you been giving her the minimum on these things, or are you generous?

➢➢ When you set the clocks ahead, ≺≺
➢➢ Check the batteries in the smoke detectors. ≺≺

March 30 Gifts/Romance

Why are there stickers everywhere?

If you regularly give her small gifts (and if you don't, why don't you) find a distinctive sticker to use as a "signature" for your gifts. When you find a good sticker (hearts are a great choice) buy a bunch and stash them away. Then put a sticker on every gift or card you give her. Buy her a candy bar, put a sticker on it, and leave it where she will find it. Get her a flower, and put the sticker on the vase. Leave her some money, with a sticker on each bill.

March 31 Touch

Why dress for bed?

Sleep naked, and encourage her to do the same. Skin on skin feels nice, and you can snuggle up better before, during, and after sleeping if you're both naked. As self-defense, suggest she wear socks if she has those wandering cold feet typical of many women.

April 01 Words

Your marriage is no April fool's joke!

Tell her, or better yet write to her, that she's no fool. Tell her that you would be a fool to not love her and care for her as the precious gift of God that she is. Throw in a "no fooling" if you like.

Hot Bonus: Ask her if she wants to fool around!

April 02 Service

WD-4 the Wife

Grab a can of WD-40 (or some similar lubricating product), and a couple of paper towels. Hit all the hinges and other sliding/moving things you can fix or improve with that miracle-of-science-in-a-can. Start with hinges, including cabinet doors. A stiff or sticky zipper will benefit from a shot, and it can remove oil and tar from clothes. WD-40 also removes the sticky mess left by labels (spray, wait, and rub off), removes crayon from wood, removes scuff marks from shoes, and works on chewing gum too. Don't forget to squirt some in all the keyholes you can find.

April 03 Time

Get away for a day.

It's always nice to get away on a private little vacation, but sometimes funds and/or time make that difficult. Still, even a single day away together can be great for your marriage, so here are some money and time saving ideas.

- If you have kids, see if you can find a couple who will trade out with you, so you can both get a break without kids.
- If you don't have kids, shoot for a weekday – motel rates are lower Sunday night thru Thursday night.
- Eating out can cost more than the motel does, so pack an ice chest and a few easy to fix foods. Have one nice meal out, and eat in the rest of the time.
- Don't go far, lest you spend too much time driving. Chances are there's someplace near you that you've never explored.
- If a hotel is out of the question, tell everyone you're taking a short vacation, and then stay at home! Turn off the phone, turn down the answering machine, close the curtains, don't check your e-mail, and ignore the world! Visit a local tourist attraction you've never had time for; or, get some movies and junk food, throw a blanket in front of the TV, and spend the day naked.

April 04 Sex

Head to Toe

Lay on your backs, side by side, with your feet at her head and her feet at your head. Adjust until your hand easily reaches between her legs and hers between yours. Now have fun; keep going until one of you "has to do more," or both of you reach orgasm.

Hot Hint: A couple of pillows under your head will give you a better view!

April 05 Holiday

Happy Birthday to Me!

Do you get what you want for your birthday? If not, maybe it's because you've not been clear about what you want. It need not be a gift that can be put in a box, you might want to ask her to join you for some event, or give you a long massage, or fix you a special meal.

Hint: If your gift request is sexual, don't use your "special day" to manipulate her into something she doesn't really want to do.

April 06 Gifts

Inflated Giving

Get her a balloon, or balloons. You might find some specialized shape like a teddy bear or a heart, or buy an assortment of colours, or get something with flowers or words like "I love you" printed on it.

Be creative about how you give balloons: leave them tied where she will find them (either at home or elsewhere), sneak by and put them in her car while she's out, or hide them in a closet. You can also use balloons as path markers to another gift; start weighted balloons near the front door and have them wander through the house with the last one tied to the gift.

Bonus: When she's coming home from a long trip or a hard day, use balloons to mark a path to a candle lit bubble bath.

April 07 Prayer

Favour

Pray for your wife to have favour with those she deals with: from her friends to people she deals with at stores, from people at church to the parents of your kid's friends, and people at work if applicable. If you have kids, especially pray that she will have favour with them.

➢➢ **She's worth it!** ≺≺

April 08 Words/Communication

I care about your feelings.
(Even when they are wrong.)

No matter how great your relationship may be, there are going to be rough spots, disagreements, and hurt feelings. When difficulties happen, remember to show her due respect by listening to both her mind and her heart. If you're not 100% sure you know what she is thinking, ask her to clarify. Be sure to honour her reality even if you don't agree with it – this will go a long way towards resolving issues and healing hurts.

April 09 Gifts

Smell Good Stuff

Women are much more scent oriented than men, so do something for her nose. Buy her a nice perfume, body wash, scented candle, or some potpourri. A bit of detective work, or a few simple questions, will help you determine which kind of scents she most enjoys.

April 10 Time

TV on Your Schedule

If there's a television show you both enjoy watching, tape it rather than watching it live. This way you can watch it when you choose, you can skip the commercials, and you don't miss things if there are interruptions. Wait until the kids are in bed, and make it a special thing that the two of you do together.

April 11 Sex

Shake things up a bit.

If you have considered trying a "sex toy," a vibrating egg or bullet is a good choice. We've heard many folks say this is the best toy or vibrator there is. In addition to being something you can use on each other, you can place the egg between your bodies during intercourse in any face-to-face position – and you will both feel the vibrations.

If this sounds like something you and your wife might want to try, check out the Christian, no porn, website listed in the on-line resources on page 213.

April 12 Service

Without asking...

Is there something she is forever reminding you to do? Is it because she's a nag, or is it because you just don't do whatever it is until/unless she asks you to? Make a commitment to yourself to take care of that thing regularly, and before she asks. Consider it a gift to her, to show how much you love her.

If you fail to do things because of forgetfulness, find ways to remind yourself. Leave notes, or put an object which reminds you of the chore where you will see it.

If there are a number of things that fit this category, work on them one at a time. When you have one down solid, then add another.

➢➢ *"Her children rise up and call her blessed"*. ≺≺
➢➢ Pr 31:28 If they don't, encourage them to! ≺≺

April 13 Touch

Be her snuggle bunny.

Snuggling just feels good, especially to a lady. On the couch or in bed, fully clothed or completely naked, curl up as close as you can, weave your arms and legs together, and hang on.

Just make sure your wife does not have cause to see snuggling as nothing more than a request for sex. It's natural for the one to lead to the other, but snuggling will not be well received if it appears that snuggling is just a way to have sex.

Hint: Make a point of doing some serious snuggling

after sex, when it will be especially well received because it's clearly not part of an "agenda."

April 14 Prayer/Walk

Watch over me and thee...

Pray for the Lord to protect your wife while you are apart, and especially while she is "out in the world." Additionally, let her know that you pray for her safety on a regular basis.

April 15 Words

I love you.

"I love you" – you cannot say it too often. Say it, write it on a card, whisper it, leave it on her voice mail, and write it on her windshield with a white board marker. Then do it again … and again.

Hot Bonus: Say it during and after sex.

Note: if you've worked on your federal income taxes in the last three days, see the tip for February 16th on page 37.

April 16 Gifts

The Key to My Heart... and the House

Buy your wife an extra house key, and find a good place to hide if for her. Avoid the "standard" key hiding places. If you have potted plants, put the key in a baggie and bury it in the edge of a pot. If you have a dog, hide the key on a hook inside the doghouse.

If you want to get fancy, you can get an

electronic door bolt that opens when you enter a code. Electronic locks, which can be purchased for under $100.00, install about as easily as a regular locksets.

April 17 Time

The dog we don't own needs a walk.

If you tend to be unaware of when she needs your time, or if she has a hard time telling you when she needs it, come up with a code phrase that she can use to indicate that her need for time with you is reaching critical. Something like, "the dog needs a walk" or, "I need your help hanging a picture" or, "the flowers are wilting" will do.

April 18 Sex/Romance

Romantic Invitation

Scatter some red rose petals on the bed to let her know you are thinking not only of sex, but also of her romantic side. To make it even nicer you can make a trail of petals leading to the bed, and arrange the petals on the bed into a heart shape.

Tip: You can pick your own petals, or buy packaged petals at a store that sells weddings things.

April 19 Service

Make the little foxes work for you.

In Song of Songs, we read, *"the little foxes spoil the vines."* Big foxes would eat fruit from the grape vines, but the little foxes, being too small to reach the fruit, and would instead chew on the stem of the vine, killing the whole plant. In much the same way, it's the little things that can hurt a relationship.

On the positive side, little things can have a huge benefit when done regularly. Pull out her chair at the table, hold a door for her, open her car door, or go get her another glass of whatever she is drinking. These are all small things, but when done regularly they add up, resulting in your wife feeling loved and cared for.

April 20 Prayer/Walk

Honey Pray List

Have your wife write down seven things about which she would like you to pray. Abbreviate the things she writes to fit on a small card (the back of a business card is great) and put it in your wallet where you will see it each time you use your wallet. Pray for these things daily, focusing on one each day of the week.

April 21 Gifts

I'll be back...

If you have to be away from home overnight, leave a gift under her pillow, or between her pillow and the bedspread. Get her a book, a candle, some candy, a book of puzzles, or whatever you know that she likes. What you give is not as important as the thought, and putting the gift where she will find it at the lonely, go-to-bed-alone time will especially bless her. Attach a card saying you miss her and will be thinking of her.

April 22 Touch

I'll scratch yours.

A nice long back scratch can be both enjoyable and relaxing. When you're in bed, get her to lie on her front, and begin a slow, gentle scratching of her entire back. Make sure you nails are not rough, and apply only moderate pressure. Keep going for a long time.

April 23 Sex/Time

The bed means sex.

Do you ever get into bed and suddenly find you can think of nothing other than sex? You know your wife needs some time to talk and connect on a non-sexual basis, and you want to give her that, but getting into bed creates a Pavlovian response that drives all non-sexual thoughts from you mind.

Learn to give her the non-sexual time she needs before you climb into bed. You could go for a walk, sit on the couch, drive to a nearby restaurant for dessert, or sit on the floor at the foot of the bed. You might even put a love seat in the bedroom; make the love seat for talking and snuggling, and the bed for sex.

Also, enlist your wife's help. Explain your dilemma to her, and ask her to help you find ways to give her what she needs to feel connected enough to be sexual.

April 24 Words

Dear Encouragement Diary....

Buy one of those blank books that can be found at bookstores and gift shops, then use it to keep a diary of the wonderful things your wife does. Don't simply write down the things she does for you, record all of the sweet, thoughtfully and godly things you see her doing for others. Keep the diary a secret for a while, and then show it to your wife. Keep adding to it, and leave it where she can see it.

April 25 Service

If it ain't completely broke....

Is there something in your home that is "sort of" broken? It works, but not quite the way it should, or as quickly or easily as it should. In your mind it may not be worth the time, effort, or money it would take to fix it for real – but does your bride feel the same way?

Most women don't find duct tape and wire repairs "charming." Either set aside some time to fix it, or bite the bullet and pay someone to take care of it.

April 26 None of the Above

If you honour her in front of others...

Lori and I regularly meet with another couple for fellowship and prayer. On one such occasion I was aware that throughout the evening the gentleman regularly touched his wife, including rubbing her feet.

How blessed that woman must have felt that her husband was not ashamed to show his love for her in front of others. I don't think he was doing it for that reason; it was just a natural expression of how he feels about his wife.

What about you; do you ever shy away from doing or saying loving things for your wife because others are around? I don't mean the "get a room" kind of things you should save for private, I mean all the little things you can say and do that demonstrate your love.

April 27 Gifts

It does grow on trees!

Get creative and give your lady a chocolate tree or bush. You will need some sort of plant with fairly rigid branches or stems, a bag of chocolate kisses, and some plastic wrap. Cut strips of plastic wrap and use them to tie the kisses to the plant.

Bonus: Make the plant something you can put in the ground after the "crop" has been harvested.

April 28 Sex/Communication

"Ya wanna do it?"

How do you communicate your desire to have sex with your wife? You may have figured out that how you ask seems to have some bearing on the answer, but are not sure how that works. On the other hand, maybe you've never thought about it.

If she is "very proper," she is not likely to respond well to slang. Slang terms that are commonly used as cursing are obviously a problem, but even more mild terms may put her off. On the other hand, asking for sex with a group of Latin words (all those "proper scientific" terms) is more likely to inspire giggling than sexual desire.

Things that affect what she does or doesn't like to hear when being asked for sex are her personality, her past, how she feels about sex, and how she feels about her own body. Also important is the message behind what you say, or more accurately (and less fairly), the message she thinks is behind what you say. Does your request indicate that you love and respect her, or does it come across as "I need sex and God only allows me do it with you"? Does what you say tell her you want her in all ways, including sexually, or does it make her feel that sex is all you want her for?

Relax, be yourself, and ask in a way that shows you care about her. Use "safe" words like "make love" or "have sex" unless you are absolutely sure she is okay with other terms. Finally, euphemisms are fine, but make sure they're not so obscure she has no idea what you are asking.

April 29 Walk

Double the Insight

If you don't study the Bible together, or even if you do, try this. Pick a book of the Bible to read at a set rate. Read separately, then later talk about what you read, what it meant to you, and how you think it applies to your life. You will often see very different things in the scriptures you read, and by sharing your insights you will get the benefit of what each of you sees.

April 30 Touch

The "Only You" Touch

Find a personal way to touch her in passing, a way no one else touches her. A quick pat on the butt, a gentle squeeze of her upper arm, or a kiss on her hand will all do nicely. As you pass her during the day, touch her, and just keep going. It's a silent "I love you."

Hint: Many women do not like to have their breasts grabbed suddenly – pick another part of her body.

May 01 Words

You can do it!

She may complain you never communicate, but sometimes we male types say too much rather than too little. You're on your own figuring out when, but there are times when what she really needs is a simple, "I know you can do it," "I trust you," or "You can handle that."

Bonus: When she is going to have to do something difficult, leave a Post-It® with one of the simple messages above where you know she will find it shortly before she has to do the task. This kind of quick message can be a great boost to her courage or confidence.

May 02 Service

Give Superwoman a Hand

Despite claims to the contrary, she is not as strong as you are. One study found that college age women who worked out with weights had lower-body strength equal to that of men who didn't work out, and upper-body strength that was less than that of men who didn't work out. Be aware of this, and give her a hand with the big jobs. Better yet, do them before she can!

May 03 Time/Romance

Wedding Memories

The next time you and your wife go to a wedding, plan to take a bit of time afterwards to walk down memory lane with her. If you live in the town you lived in when you were engaged and/or married you could take a tour of important places: where you proposed, where you spent time together, where you first kissed, and where you were married. If you live in another town, pull out the wedding album and take a tour that way. Finish off with a nice meal, and tell her how glad you are to be married to her.

May 04 Sex

Naked Twister

The folks at Hasbro still make the game Twister®. Go buy a set and play some naked twister with your bride! One extra rule, before a person can spin, he or she must kiss some nearby part of the other's body.

May 05 Holiday

Mother's Day

Mother's Day is the second Sunday in May.

If she has children, be sure to honour her on mother's day; if her children are still at home, make sure they honour her too! Flowers are always a good choice, and a corsage for church might be a great choice. Lunch out after church is nice, but it can be crowded and hectic. Instead, make (and clean up) a nice meal at home, or pack a picnic basket. (See the food section on page 190 for cooking help.)

Tip: If you struggle with infertility, this can be a very difficult day for her. Let her know you will do whatever you can to help. If she just can't face church that day, it's not a sin to miss a Sunday for her sake. Take her out for brunch, and make sure she knows how much you love her.

If she is not yet a mother, or is not a mother by choice, may I suggest that the two of you do something for a single mother in your church or community. Take her out to lunch, give her a really nice gift (gift certificates for things she needs, or things she would never buy for herself), or offer to provide some free baby-sitting.

May 06 Touch

Touched by a Diner

Make a point of touching her when you eat together. Brief contact with her hand, a touch of her face, and don't forget foot contact. This is especially good when you are dining out alone, but try to make it a regular part of every meal.

May 07 Service

Vacuums Suck

Do something practical. Launder some clothes, wash some dishes, vacuum the floor, or clean one of the bathrooms.

Be aware of when your wife is especially busy, tired, or overwhelmed, this is an ideal time to do practical things for her.

Hint: Occasionally do some of these things for no reason at all – it never hurts to keep her guessing!

May 08 Gifts

Hidden Gifts

Buy several small inexpensive gifts – her favorite candy, a knick-knack, a small candle, or anything else you know she would like. Wrap the items all the same way, or put them in matching gift bags, and add a small tag with her name. Label the gifts "1 of 6," "2 of 6," and so on. Now "hide" the gifts in out-of-the-way places where she will come across them – the refrigerator, her lingerie drawer, hanging from the bathtub faucet, the front seat of her car, or under her pillow. Be creative, and have fun blessing her!

May 09 Prayer/Sex

"Uh God, about sex..."

Have you ever prayed about sex? (I'm not talking about "Oh God, let her say yes.") Have you ever prayed about your sex life as a couple? Many of us have a hard time reconciling sex and prayer, but God cares about our sex lives, and He wants us to bring everything to Him in prayer. So, no matter what sexual problems you might have, or if you just want a good sex life to be better, grab your wife and pray about your love life.

You should pray about sexual issues on your own. Pray that you will be able to discern what will really pleasure her, and pray for the ability to give her those things. You can pray about impotence or premature ejaculation or her difficulty in reaching climax. It's even okay to pray for more sex, and you can certainly pray for her to think about and have feelings about sex, and to act on those feelings in a manner consistent with God's will. Pray for her to desire sex, to be aroused by you, and to enjoy your lovemaking.

May 10 Words

"I just called, to say..."

Phone her from work, and tell her something she did recently that blessed and/or impressed you. Better yet, make a point of calling every day this week to encourage her in this way. There's no need for long speeches or flowery words, just offer a simple message of love and encouragement.

May 11 Time

Booth-by-Booth Date

Go to a flea market or a craft/artist fair. Walk hand in hand, laugh together about strange things you see, and buy something to remind you of your time together. When you're walked out, stop for a drink and a snack on a bench or under a tree.

May 12 Service

Be Mister Easy Off

Sometime when she's going to be gone for a while, clean the oven for her. It's not complicated; just follow the directions on the can of cleaner you buy. Don't forget to do the burners.

May 13 Sex

Lunch at a motel?

See if you can arrange a workday "lunch date" with your wife at a nearby motel.

Hint: Pack a sandwich to eat on the way back to work!

May 14 Gifts

Get her something she didn't know she couldn't live with out.

Go to the supermarket of discount store and shop the kitchen gadget aisle. There are all kinds of weird and wonderful things there, and you can probably find something she will not only use, but also come to wonder how she lived with out. A couple of such items – a microwave hard-boiled egg maker and an electric jar opener.

May 15 Touch

Red Light Hand Signals

When you're in the car together, reach over and hold her hand at all the stoplights. Don't say or do anything else out of the ordinary, just hold her hand for the duration, and give a little squeeze before you let go.

➢➢ She's worth it! ≺≺

May 16 Time/Romance

BYOE

BYOE – that's Bring Your Own Elegance. Have a fancy, elegant meal at Taco Bell® or Burger King®. Carefully pack some nice dishes and silverware in a bag or backpack. Add candles, a tablecloth, a bud vase with a flower, and so on. When you get to the eatery, order your food, and then set the table while you wait for your order to be called.

Tip: If you go when the restaurant is not busy, and buy their food, they should have any problem with your additions.

May 17 Prayer/Walk

Got Fellowship?

Do you love the Lord, but can't find a church that seems to be what you think church should be? If so, you are not alone, there are a growing number of "unchurched Christians." It's estimated that in the USofA there are 12.5 million who have a deep relationship with the Lord, but no longer go to church. Worldwide the number is over 100 million – and growing fast. New Zealand pastor Alan Jamieson said about these people, "Many of them said that they left the church not because they had lost their faith, but exactly because they did not want to lose it."

If this is you, or you feel you're headed this way, don't throw out the fellowship with the church. Christian fellowship is vital, without it we're like a lone sheep, easy prey for the wolf. Find some other "followers of Jesus" and spend regular time with them. Do a Bible study, get together for prayer, or simply meet together regularly for meals and fellowship. Whatever you do, stay connected!

For more on "Out-of-church Christians" see www.house2house.tv/index.pl/articles/00070. Other pages of the same web site talk about home church, a growing movement that some who've left formal churches are very excited about.

May 18 Sex

Regular Guys, Amazing Sex

Over the years, I've talked to some happily married men who seem extraordinary in what they can do sexually. Maybe they are unusual, but I suspect a bigger factor is that they are open to the possibility of things most of us think to be impossible. I think we hear the "experts" tell us what to expect, and these become self-imposed limits. You know, the kind of limits I'm talking about: "after 30 you can forget about twice in one night," "after 50 you can forget about two days in a row," "after 70 you can forget about it altogether." My challenge here is to ditch all those limits, and find what your own body can and can not do.

First a bit of biology: Men (but not women) have something called the "refractory period." This is often wrongly defined as the period of time after an orgasm during which a man cannot have another erection. In truth, the refractory period is the period of time after climax when a man cannot climax again. It may seem a subtle difference, but it's not. I've spoken to several fellows who can climax during intercourse, stay firm enough to keep going, and ejaculate a second time 10 to 20 minutes later. Other men don't ejaculate again, but can keep going for a good long while. Still other men lose their erection, but are able to regain enough of an erection for intercourse in a matter of minutes. You can see how a wife might see any of these as a very good thing!

Now for some examples: These come from men I know well enough to trust that they are telling the truth. All of the "extraordinary sex" I'm describing was accomplished by men who were over forty, with their wife of more than ten years. None of this is "male multiple orgasm" – it's all individual, separate ejaculations.

Several of the men were able to have six to

eight climaxes in 24 hours. One fellow had intercourse six times a day for six days in a row. Several of the men were able to climax twice in half an hour, one three times in less than an hour, one twice in less than fifteen minutes. Finally, one man in his seventies is still having sex with his wife almost every night!

If these guys are rather unique, then these facts mean nothing to you and I; but I am convinced these men are not unique. I think most men could do similar things if they only believed they could.

Consider the middle-aged man who goes on a business trip and ends up committing adultery with a woman half his age. He has more sex in a couple of days than he would have with his wife in a couple of weeks. He does things like those described above for the first time in his life. What was different that "allowed" the man to do those things? He had the same body he has when he is sexual with his wife. Is there an excitement about someone new or "forbidden sex," that allowed him to do things he never did before? Maybe he tried harder because he was desperate to impress the young lady? Whatever the cause, **it is all in his mind**. His body is clearly been capable of extraordinary sex; it's his mind that's been limiting him. Of course, I'm not advocating adultery – I've seen the devastation adultery causes to everyone involved, including innocent children. My point is that the difference is in the guy's mind, not his pants!

My suggestion is to forget what you think you know about male sexual limits. Forget about what the sexperts say is normal or usual. Forget about the limits on sexuality you have read about or heard. Focus on your wife, and your love and desire for her, and don't limit yourself.

May 19 Service

If you want to help, DON'T HELP!

As much as she wants and needs your help, there are times when you may be more of a hindrance than a help. Sometimes it's because you're getting in her way, and sometimes it's because she knows how she wants it done and it's easier to do it than to try to explain it to you. Learn when to back out graciously; if you ask if you can help, and she says no, maybe she means it!

➢➢ **How long since you gave her flowers?** ≺≺

May 20 None of the above

I was wrong (this time).

"Therefore if you bring your gift to the altar, and there remember that your brother has something against you, leave your gift there before the altar, and go your way. First be reconciled to your brother, and then come and offer your gift." (Matthew 5:23-24)

When you blow it, do you apologize? When you're wrong, do you admit it? Some of us were raised to see apologizing or admitting error as a sign of weakness, but Jesus does not seem to agree.

In reality, there is a benefit to being able to apologize or admit that you were wrong – when you do insist you're right, your wife can't dismiss it as your "typical pride and hard headedness." When you were wrong, admit you were. When you've acted wrongly, apologize.

May 21 Gifts

Celebrate Hug a Book Lover Day or Great Butt Day

Invent some holidays as an excuse to give your wife gifts. You can use your made-up holidays to let her know what you like about her, or to honour one of her hobbies or interests. Get creative and find gifts to match the holiday (a gift certificate for a bookstore or thong panties for the two in the subject line). If she enjoys it, make notes and be sure to celebrate each holiday annually!

May 22 Touch

Follicle Fondling

Give your wife a scalp massage. Stand or sit behind her, and place your hands on either side of her head with your fingers spread as if you were holding a basketball with your fingertips. Your thumbs should be on the back of her head, your pinkies just in front of her ears. Rub with your fingers as you slowly move your hands in small circles. Slowly rotate your hands so your thumbs are at her neck and your pinkies are over her ears.

May 23 Time/Communication

20 (or more) Questions

Each of you comes up with a list of questions – things you don't know about each other. Then you take turns asking each other. Anything you ask her you have to be ready to answer yourself, and vice versa.

In addition to all those burning questions you have, ask some questions that will help you better bless your wife in the future; things like her favourite candy, favourite colours, what kind of clothing she likes, and so on.

May 24 Words

I really like how you look.

Studies have found – no surprise here – that virtually all women are concerned they don't "look good enough." This is no small issue – it can devastate a woman, cause her to avoid certain situations, or result in her husband never seeing her fully naked! Society is daily telling your wife she is too fat, that her breasts are too small, that her hair is too flat, that her complexion is bad, that she is too wrinkled, and so on, and so on, and so on.

You may be the only voice telling her that she is beautiful, desirable, and not deserving of having a paper bag put over her head. Your voice against the world ... you're in the minority, so you'll have to work very hard to convince her that your reality is the truth. Keep at it – it will have an effect.

May 25 Sex

Sound Off!

Have you ever suspected your wife is holding back vocally during sex? Certainly not all women are "screamers" but a certain amount of noise is a normal part of sex, and very few women are completely quiet just because that's how they're wired. Often silence is a result of "nice girls don't do that" thinking or it could be that she is afraid of what you would think if she made noise. If you think these are issues for your wife, discuss them.

Another common concern for women is that someone else in the house will hear. One way to coax her to worry about noise less, without even mentioning it, is to provide background noise so she won't be self-conscious about every heavy breath. Music is one time-tested way to go – consider the beat and tempo, you don't want to put her to sleep. Instrumentals are good, or you can try some "sounds of nature" CD's.

If kids are the issue, you can play the music in your room, in their rooms (young children) or in the living room if it's between you and them. Another option is to run just the fan on the central air/heat, creating a nice white noise. Even if this doesn't result in more noise from your wife, both of you may feel freer if you aren't concern about being overheard.

May 26 Romance

Crouching Romance, Hidden Roses.

Touch her romantic side by leaving a red rose, or a bunch of them, somewhere unexpected. She might find them in a basket full of laundry, or in her lingerie drawer, or in the cabinet where the coffee is kept. Try to place the flowers shortly before they will be found, so they will be fresh.

Bonus: If there's some situation she's struggling with,

or that has been getting her down, try to place the flowers where they will be connected with the difficult issue or task. If the baby won't sleep, leave them where she will find them when she has to go rock the baby yet again. If she is studying for something very difficult, leave the flowers by her books.

May 27 Service

Don't sweat the big stuff.

Is there something your wife regularly buys that is big, bulky, and/or heavy? It could be bottled water, big bags of dog food, or industrial sized containers of laundry detergent. Make a point of getting those items for her. Don't wait for her to run out, keep an eye on the item, and buy a replacement before she goes shopping.

May 28 Gifts

Gathered from All Over the World

Are you going on vacation this year? Start a collection of something you can buy at each of your vacations from now on. It could be souvenir plates, or post cards, or some non-souvenir item you both like that would be available in any gift shop. If it's not obvious from the item, make a note of where you bought it on the bottom.

Tip: If you have to travel without her, be sure to add to the collection and give it to her as a gift when you get home.

May 29 Touch

A Bite for You, a Bite for Me

Try feeding her finger foods. Touch her lips and face a lot more than necessary, and kiss away any food that does not go where it should.

May 30 Time

Left Feet and All

Take dance lessons together. Go all out and learn some ballroom dancing! Lot's of fun, great exercise, and plenty of togetherness.

May 31 Words

I'd still marry you.

Have you recently told her how much you love and appreciate her? Have you told her why you love her, what it is about her (other than her body) that impresses and blesses you? Have you told her you would marry her all over again?

June 01 Sex

Maybe she has not because she asks not.

In theory, all women can have multiple orgasms. In reality, some don't have them because they don't want them, and others think that they are more effort than they are worth; but there are also women who've never thought to try, or are too shy to ask. Without making it seem like you expect it, let her know you would be glad to experiment and see if she can have more climaxes.

June 02 Prayer

Lest God cut us off...

A challenging verse:

"Husbands, likewise, dwell with them with understanding, giving honor to the wife, as to the weaker vessel, and as being heirs together of the grace of life, that your prayers may not be hindered." (One Peter 3:7)

Peter says that an improper attitude toward our wife can hinder our prayers. The Greek word rendered as "hindered" is *Ekkopto*, and it literally means, "cut off". Most of the uses of this word in the New Testament indicate pruning or cutting down of a plant. So, if we are not acting rightly toward our wife, the Lord "cuts off" our prayers. Sounds like God is very interested in how we treat our wife, and it sounds like doing it His way is more important than doing what is "politically correct," what we feel like doing, or even what our wife thinks would make her most happy.

All of this is to make the point that we should each spend more than a little time praying about how we treat our wife and how we **should be** treating her. Certainly, we need her feedback, but ultimately we will answer to the Lord for the kind of husband we were on this earth. The ultimate act of generosity is to treat our wife the way God wants us to treat her!

June 03 Gifts

That's a Wrap!

Part of the fun of receiving gifts is unwrapping them. Even if it's a small, simple gift, wrapping it up makes it more special. If you can't wrap, don't worry – stock up on small printed cardboard boxes, pre-made bows, ribbon, gift bags, and coloured tissue paper.

June 04 Service

School's Out!

If you have school age kids, the summer break puts an extra load on your wife, so find a way to give her a break each week. Stay home with the kids while she "runs away," or take the kids so she can have some alone time at home.

Tip: Even if your children are homeschooled, the summer can be tough with more friends over and your children wanting to go more places.

➢➢ *"It is not good that man should be alone."* Ge 2:18 ≺≺

June 05 Touch

Face Time

Take turns slowly touching each other's face. Sit down on the floor or the couch, and have her lay to one side with her head in your lap. Have her close her eyes while you slowly and gently explore her entire face (include the ears) with your fingers. Switch.

June 06 Sex

Get Grounded

If you have sex in the "missionary position," you can make it easier, more comfortable, and quite possibly much better for both of you, by making sure your feet are against something solid. Doing this makes it easier on your arms, allows you to put less weight on her, and puts you in a position that should feel a bit better to her. By lessening tension in your leg and buttock muscles, this may also allow you to last longer. If your bed doesn't have a footboard, try putting the pillows at the other end of the bed and put your feet against the headboard or the wall.

➢➢ **She's worth it!** ≺≺

June 07 Time

2 for 1 vacation

If you have occasion to travel for business, try to get your wife to join you. If you're driving, your only extra expenses will be food. If you are flying, think of it as one free plane fare and the motel being paid for. Of course, you have to work a good deal of the time, but you can find some local attraction for her to visit during the day, and then spend time together in the evenings.

Tip: Try adding a day or two to the beginning or end of your trip for a real vacation. Look for a break on room rates or airfare based on the longer trip.

June 08 Words

"If it were not for you..."

Be honest, you're a better person because of her, aren't you? She softens your rough edges, and fills in where you are lacking. You have each benefited from the other, and both of you has become more balanced. Tell her how much her loving input into your life has helped and improved you.

June 09 Gifts

Pink Toolbox

Get her a toolbox that is all hers. You might be able to find a prepackaged set – I got one with "girl size tools" in a powder blue case. If you can't find it ready made, buy a small plastic toolbox, and stock it yourself. Put in all the tools she might need. Be sure to include small nails and some tape.

Hint: If you have kids, tell them using mom's tools is a good way to get in big trouble.

June 10 Holiday/ Romance

Remember your MIL on your wife's birthday.

Send your mother-in-law flowers on your wife's birthday. Yes, you read that correctly. If you attach a card, a simple "thank you" is enough. Trust me, word of what you've done will get back to your wife, and you will end up blessing two women with one gift.

June 11 Service

While you were away...

Next time she is out of town for a day or more, do something around the house that will bless her. Fix or replace something (or be there for a repairman to do it). Clean out the garage, attic, or junk closet. Cut down a dead tree, cut back the shrubs, or fix the fence.

Tip: Don't blow it by leaving her a pile of dirty clothes or dishes!

June 12 Touch

Handy

Any time you're sitting with her or sitting across from her at a table, take her hand. Hold it, stroke it, and trace her fingers with yours. Let it be a lingering touch that says, "I love you."

June 13 Walk

Being all she can be in His army.

The very best thing you can do for your wife is to encourage her to be what God's called her to be. Pray with and for her to know His will, and to discover the gifts He's given her. Talk with her about what kind of ministry she feels she should be pursuing, and be quick to support her efforts to learn, grow, and move toward that.

Tip: If you have children at home, especially small

ones, your wife may feel she will never be anything "more than" a mother. While mothering is clearly one of the most important ministries any woman can have, it is likely that God will call her to other ministries. Even if she's not yet able, be sure to pray with her about future ministry, and help her to prepare now.

June 14 Sex

TAKE ME!

The reason bodice ripper romances are so popular is many women like to be "taken" sexually. Not raped, but urgently taken by a man who just has to have her NOW! Of course, that statement is not politically correct, and it may be a problem for a woman with sexual or physical abuse in her past, but the reality is many women enjoy being desired in a way that leads to "being taken." If you're not sure how your wife feels about this, talk to her about it.

If you decide to give it a try, start small and work up as you see how it goes. A few torn blouse buttons or tearing off her panties may have a major impact on her. You may both be surprised by how much "being taken" arouses her.

June 15 Prayer

Pray for the fatherless.

Father's Day is the third Sunday in June.

Father's Day is approaching – bad neckties, homemade gifts, and indistinguishable breakfasts will abound. But what of the millions upon millions of children around the world who have no father to love... or to be loved by? These children are at a great disadvantage in so many ways. Please prayer for the fatherless – may they find the true Father of us all, and be comforted and blessed by Him.

Don't forget the fatherless in your own church. Be a blessing to the kids without dads, and to their single mothers. Don't be stingy with your time, or your treasure, when it comes to these kids.

➢➢ *"Marriage is honorable among all."* He 13:4a ➢➢

June 16 Gifts

Flat, Plastic Gifts

Gift cards are becoming very common –they look like a credit card, and you can put any amount of money on them. Buy your wife a gift card for a clothing store, a book or music store, or the movies. Some malls sell gift cards that can be used in any shop in the mall. Put the gift card in a card, put her name on the envelope, and leave where she will find it.

June 17 Touch

A Different Kind of Massage

Have her lie naked, face down on the bed, and cover her with just a sheet. Give her a foot to head massage through the sheet. Then have her turn over and work from the top down on the front side, again through the sheet. The sensation for her will be different, and you might learn something new about her body.

Hot Bonus: If she seems interested, massage her to orgasm through the sheet.

June 18 Time

Time Out

If there are certain times of the year when you are very busy, or certain projects that eat up a lot of time, schedule in some "time outs" with your wife. I do mean schedule, write them in your date book, let her know ahead of time when you plan to "hang out" with her, and make it your most important appointment of the day.

Grab a few choice snacks and go spend some time with your wife in some quiet, private place in the house. Talk a bit, share your love verbally, and toss in a foot or shoulder massage. Even fifteen minutes like this will go a long way to showing her that she really is important to you. While it's not all the time she wants or deserves, it can serve as a promissory note for more time when things slow down.

June 19 Service

Fill in as Needed

When you see her getting behind, for whatever reason, take up some of the slack. Offer to do something that she normally does, or just do it. Just make sure you know how to do it and do it right! This can be anything from childcare, to bill paying, to chores, to playing chauffeur.

Hint: Don't point it out, and don't look to be thanked. In addition, if you receive praise, say it's just 'cause you love her.

June 20 Words

Rewind, Stop, Play ... Rewind, Stop, Play...

Record a cassette tape telling your wife how wonderful she is. It need not be long, and it need not be polished prose, just tell her what you like about her. If the car she drives has a cassette player, put your tape in and set it to play when she starts the car. In the house, put the tape in the cassette player and leave a "hit play" note.

Hint: If you have the tools and the knowledge, you can do the same thing on CD. Alternatively, you can record a wave file on her computer and set it to run at a given time or event (like start up) or when she clicks an icon on her desktop.

June 21 Sex/Communication

Hints are for guessing games.

Hints do not qualify as adequate sexual communication! Too often, hints lead to hurt feelings because the person on the receiving end either misses or misinterprets the hints. For example, a man may think he is being very clear about his desire to have sex, while his wife is clueless, resulting in him being mad that she didn't "say yes," and her being confused about why he's upset.

Be clear about what you want, and how you want it. Don't hide your desires within an excess of words, and don't use flowery terms or unclear euphemisms. If she does not know what you are asking, she can't do it no matter how much she might like to please you.

June 22 Touch

Here's mud in your eye!

Go to the cosmetic/beauty section of the local supermarket or drug store and buy a mud mask. Read the directions until you know them by heart, and then give your wife a facial. In general, application means washing her face, patting it dry, applying the mud (avoiding the nostrils and lips), letting it dry, and rinsing it of completely.

Tip: While she's waiting for you to wash it off, give her a shoulder rub.

June 23 Time

You are invited...

Invite your wife to a meal out, but do it up right. Send her a formal invitation with something like "The pleasure of your company is requested at (restaurant) for a fine meal on (date) at (time)." Enclose an RSVP card and a stamped, addressed envelope.

Hot Bonus: Have a matching invitation to give her at the restaurant, this time requesting the pleasure of her company in the bedroom!

June 24 Walk

A Hard Study

Mention headship and obedience to any group of Christians and you will get a variety of opinions, some of them just short of violent. Without "giving away" my opinion here, consider that the Bible says we are to treat our wife as Christ treats the church. If you want to be a better husband, study what the Bible shows us about Christ, and figure out how you can apply these things to your relationship with your wife.

June 25 Service

Stylish Cool

Make some fancy ice cubes to put in all those drinks you bring her (you do bring her all those drinks, don't you?). Just place something fancy in each spot in a standard ice tray, and fill with hot water – from the tap – to ensure clear cubes. Freeze and serve. The cubes look especially nice in a tall, clear glass of water.

Fancy ice ideas:

- Whole berries (raspberries are great)
- Fresh mint leaves (good for tea)
- Grapes
- Melon balls
- Maraschino cherries (get green and red,)
- Thin slices of orange, lime or lemon.

June 26 Gifts

Across the Miles

You can get some extra mileage out of a gift by giving it publicly. Your goal here is to make her feel special in front of her friends, not to embarrass her, so subtlety is the key. Rather than showing up in person and making a big deal, send or leave a single flower some place where she will find it when she is with a couple of her girl friends. It should be easy to get one of her friends to help you, if need be.

Once when my wife went to a women's conference, I gave one of the other women from our church a silk rose with instructions to leave it on her pillow at the conference. Be creative, and you can bless her even when you are miles apart.

June 27 Words

Snail Mail from her Male

In this day of Instant Messages and e-mail, an "ordinary" card in the post box stands out. Buy her a card, write a few words about how much you love her and how wonderful she is, and mail it.

June 28 Sex

Clean up what you mess up.

Sex can be a bit messy (if it's not, you may not be doing it right!). To make clean up easy, buy some clean up towels and keep them in the night table drawer. Terry cloth hand towels are good, and if you can find them, terry cloth napkins are even better because they are softer and just the right size.

Tip: Buy colours that coordinate with the colours in the bedroom.

June 29 Prayer

Sticks and stones are nothing...

The saying goes "sticks and stones may break my bones, but words will never hurt me." A nice thought maybe, but in reality, words can do a great deal of damage, and that damage can last for a very long time. Pray for your wife about any wounding she has received because of the words of those around her.

June 30 Time

Shot Gun!

When there is an errand to run, do you go together, or do you maximize your time by one of you going and one of you staying home to do something else? Going alone may be wise management of time, but going together may be a much better use of your time. A few minutes alone together in the car can help you feel better connected.

July 01 Touch

Soap Massage

Take a shower together, and wash each other. A soapy back lends itself to a nice massage, so stand her in front of the hot water and massage until she is so relaxed she's in danger of falling.

➢➢ Love ≺≺

"Love suffers long and is kind; love does not envy; love does not parade itself, is not puffed up; 5 does not behave rudely, does not seek its own, is not provoked, thinks no evil; 6 does not rejoice in iniquity, but rejoices in the truth; 7 bears all things, believes all things, hopes all things, endures all things."

➢➢ 1 Corinthians 13:4-7 ≺≺

July 02 Service

"Maybe that would look better over there..."

Does your wife like to rearrange the furniture? Maybe she wants some new pictures hung on the wall? Loan her some time and some muscles, and let her play with the way thing are arranged.

Tip: Don't roll your eyes when she wants to vacuum a spot of rug that is about to be covered by the couch!

July 03 Words/Romance

Phony phone messages

Go to an office supply store and buy a small phone-message pad. Put it by the phone, and leave fake messages for your wife.

Examples:

- "Your beautician called – said she can't improve on perfection and canceled your appointment."
- "Some guy named (your name) called; I think he has a crush on you."
- "(Name of your child's school) called – wanted you to know they think you are a great mother."
- "The guy you were with last night left a message... WOW and THANK YOU!"

July 04 Sex

Bedroom Fireworks?

Are you interested in trying oral sex on your wife, but unsure of how she will react? Try this:

Step 1: Discuss the idea some time when you are not having, or about to have sex. Make sure she doesn't think it's wrong or gross.

Step 2: While having sex, give her a few kisses on the genitals. No tongue, no lingering, just kiss her, and move on. Do **not** immediately ask her how she liked it!

Step 3: On another occasion try something a bit more

stimulating, and for a bit longer, as part of foreplay. Again, do it for a short period, and then move on.

Step 4: Talk again, when sex is not imminent, and see how she is feeling about it. See if she would like more oral sex in foreplay, or if she is interested in having an orgasm that way.

Hint: If she says, "How would you feel if I did it to you?" don't yell too loudly.

July 05 Gifts

Throw Away Dishes

Buy some paper plates (not the thin flimsy stuff, get some with a bit of body), paper napkins, plastic cups, and plastic "silverware." Wrap it up and add a card that says it's for when she feels too tired, stressed, or grumpy to face having to do any dishes. Replace as she uses them up.

July 06 Communication

No Secrets - Past, Present or Future

Do you know all about her past? Does she know all about yours? Do you share what happens to you daily, from the mundane to the embarrassing?

If we are trying to "be one" as God says we should be, we have to share everything about ourselves. Any part of you that is not shared is an obstacle to the oneness that God has called you and your wife to have. Likewise, for any part of her that she is not sharing with you.

Yes, this kind of total disclosure is difficult – it makes you vulnerable, and at first it can be very uncomfortable. On the other hand, imagine sharing all of yourself and finding complete love and acceptance.

July 07 Time

"Who are you, and what have you done with my husband?"

Hate to shop? Hate to watch your wife shop even more? Okay, it's a normal guy thing to dislike shopping – but enjoying shopping is a normal gal thing, and wanting you to go along and give advice she will ignore is normal too. So suck it up and go shopping with her. Carry her stuff, sit in the dreaded "husband chair," and share an ice cream or soda.

Fun Tip: If want to mess with her mind say, "I think you need some new shoes – let's go shopping!"

July 08 Service

A Token of My Love

Find some kind of "token" to leave behind when you do something for her. The token can be a certain sticker (remember the shiny stars from grade school), or a game chip (buy a bunch of small ones at a toy store), or even a specific bolt or washer.

Leave your token when you clean something, put something up, or fix something for your wife.

July 09 Words

You've got encouraging e-mail!

A pastor friend sent me the following with permission to share it here:

Last fall, I made a commitment to myself that I would send my wife an e-mail everyday to let her know I loved her. Just to be sure I wouldn't be "too busy" or distracted from doing this, I placed a reminder in my calendar in Outlook (Yahoo Calendar does the same thing) so that every morning when I got to work, it would pop up, where it stays until I send that message.

Usually, the note is a paragraph, sometimes less, sometimes more. I try to think of something special she has done in the last 24 hours and let her know how I appreciate her. Other days, I might comment on our lovemaking from that morning or the night before. Or, if she looked really hot in the shower as I left for work, I'd just tell her that.

Some days require more effort than others, usually when I'm really busy or stressed out about stuff, but I find it "grounding" to take a minute and reflect on the blessing she is to me. I make it a point to never include any other "stuff" in my email. In other words, I don't remind her to take the car for an oil change, or tell her what groceries we're missing. If those things need to be said, I send them in a separate email, even if it means sending two messages back-to-back. It would be easy to "cheat" and send a message like that and say, "I love you" at the end (as I always do), and count that as my email, but I won't.

July 10 Sex

How much is enough?

One of the most common sexual problems we hear is a husband and wife with very different sex drives. One thing that can make this problem difficult to resolve is thinking of "sex" as requiring intercourse. I'm not saying intercourse is unimportant, but there are other ways to be sexual that can result in pleasure for both of you, and release for the one with the stronger drive. Manual or oral sex can be very pleasurable, and do not require as much effort for the person who is not feeling like being sexual.

If "mismatched desire" is an issue in your marriage, talk with your wife about these options. Discuss the situation, and find ways of meeting the needs each of you has.

Nag: While it's not as common, there are couples where the woman has a stronger drive than the man. If this is the case for you, make a commitment to give your wife everything she wants, even if there are times when it's "just for her." Failing to meet a woman's sexual needs is one of the most painful, damaging, and unloving things a man can do to his wife.

July 11 Gifts/Romance

A Sweet Love Note

Use her favourite candy to spell out a message on the bed. "I love you," "Forever," "WOW!" or whatever works for you.

July 12 Touch

Which parts are non-sexual?

You've heard all about the importance of giving your wife non-sexual touch, but, as a guy, her whole body is sexual to you, right? Part of it is intent, but to her touching some areas is always sexual, while other areas normally are not. Want to know which are which? Get her to show you. This exercise will help you learn where you can touch without being accused of trying to start something.

Have her put on a T-shirt and pants, and then lie face down on the bed or floor. Move your hand over her body, and ask her to rate how sexual the touch is on a scale from zero (not at all sexual) to five (the most sexual). Then have her roll over and do the same on her front side. Then it's her turn to do you, with you telling her which of your parts you find are most and least sexual for her to touch.

Hot Bonus: You will probably find some sexual spots on her body of which you were not aware. Add these to your foreplay focus.

➢➢ Who's body is it? ≺≺

"The wife does not have authority over her own body, but the husband does. And likewise the husband does not have authority over his own body, but the wife does." 1Co 7:4

➢➢ ≺≺

July 13 Prayer

A Prayer of Gratitude

When she's near enough to hear, say, "God, thank you for the great wife you gave me!" We're supposed to thank the Lord for what He has done for us, and it will bless your wife.

Hot Bonus: If she won't think it blasphemy, try the same prayer right after some particularly great sex.

July 14 Service

Trash Talk

Recently I was reading the comments of a number of ladies talking about their least liked chores at home - every one of them expressing how very much they hate to take the trash out. While it's probably not universal, I got the feeling that for a good number of women, trash removal is rather high on the list of jobs they really, really don't want to do. So...

July 15 Gifts

Shop Now, Give Later

Any time you are out with your wife, keep an eye on what she is interested in. When you see something she really likes, go back later and buy it for the next gift-giving occasion, no matter how far in the future that might be. This is especially good with a unique item – she will be so impressed to receive it months later, and will be blessed to know you were thinking of her so far in advance.

July 16 Words

1:1 just won't do.

A study of marriages found that good marriages have a compliment to complaint ratio of ten to one, or better. There are times when we need to "complain," and we should not neglect telling our wife about things that bother us, but we need to balance that. Unless there are many compliments for each complaint, the complaints will not be well received, and it's unlikely they will be acted on. Keep score of your compliment to complaint ratio, and make changes as needed.

July 17 Sex/Communication

Talking, the Other Kind of Intercourse

Many couples, even couples with fairly good sex lives, just don't talk about sex. This can cause a variety of problems, and can result in both husband and wife being needlessly frustrated.

Sometimes couples don't talk about sex because they think Christians shouldn't talk about such things. Another reason for silence is fear of what our spouse might think about what we think about sex. Basic shyness and lack of a good sexual vocabulary can also prevent good sexual communication. Whatever the block, take the lead in dealing with it so you can discuss this important area of your life.

Real life example: Once when my wife and I were ministering to a couple, he privately confided to me that he wanted to try other positions, but knew she would be unwilling. Meanwhile, his wife was telling my wife that she wanted to try other positions, but knew he was opposed to it. After Lori and I compared notes we nudged them to discuss it, and they were both pleasantly surprised.

What might you and your wife both want, but be afraid that the other would reject? It's usually best to discuss sex some time other than when you are making love or are about to make love – after sex works for some, not for others. Go slowly, give each other room, and be willing to give her time to mull over what's said before commenting on it.

July 18 Touch

Surrounded by Comfort

Think of ways to put more softness and comfort in her daily life – fuzzy slippers, T-sheets for the bed (feel like a T-shirt, soft and thick), a soft robe, even extra soft toilet tissue and Kleenex®. Look for ways to pamper her by indulging her enjoyment of soft, comfortable things.

July 19 Time

Hometown Tourist

Play tourist in your own town by going the places tourist go. Make a day of it; stroll through some shops, buy a souvenir, even take some "we were here" type pictures.

July 20 Gifts

Candy with a Surprise Inside

Buy a container for candy – something clear like a nice jar. Fill with candy your wife likes – the smaller the pieces the better. Hide a special gift in the center of the jar.

July 21 Service

Make sure she is not the least or last.

Are there little acts of service you do for people at work, or church, or elsewhere that you rarely or never do for your wife? Be sure she gets all that you give others, plus some!

July 22 Words

Public Blessing

I attended a conference where one fellow stood up and publicly blessed several of the people in attendance, finishing with his wife. He thanked her for being there with him, spoke of how much she blessed him, how she made him a better man, how much he liked her laugh, and more. I could not see his wife from my seat, but I noticed that many of the women in the room had tears in their eyes.

There's a very real spiritual component to blessing someone, particularly when it is done in front of others. Additionally, you can also encourage other couples to grow by modeling this kind of love.

July 23 Walk

Get Versed

Do you know your wife's favourite scripture? How about her favourite book of the Bible, her favourite chapter or passage? Does she know yours? Talk about what your favourites are, and why you like them.

July 24 Sex

Show and Tell

Even if your wife would make "Miss July" look ugly, chances are she worries about how her body looks, and fears that you are not truly "turned-on" by her. Try showing her how untrue this is by slowly undressing her in front of a mirror, and telling her how you see her body. Touch and stroke each area as you tell her how that part arouses you, how you think about it during the day, how a glimpse of it makes you want her, and how glad you are that her very sexy body is yours.

Bonus: Has your wife ever really seen that part of her you like so much? A fair number of adult women have never viewed their genitals with a mirror, and don't really know what they look like. With a hand mirror and some loving patience, you may be able to help her understand her body better, and feel better about her body and sexuality. Go slowly, and give her time and space to take is all in. You might want to comment on what you both see, depending on how you think she will react. If she seems to think her sex organs are funny looking, "gross" or ugly, assure her that they are very beautiful to you.

July 25 Gifts

The Gift Box

Get a nice looking box the size of a large shoebox; you want a removable top, or a pull out drawer. You may find something ready made in the stationary section of your local Wal*Mart® (or similar store) or you can "fancy it up" yourself. Add a label to the box that reads "Gift Box."

Put the box in your bedroom where you know your wife will see it. Leave it empty for a day or so, and then slip a small gift into it. Add gifts at irregular intervals; put in gifts a couple days in a row, then nothing for a few days, then every other day.

The gifts need not be expensive or fancy. If you notice she is about out of something, such as her shampoo, it will do nicely for a gift. Things like bookmarks or socks or paperback books all work, and don't forget the chocolate.

Hot Bonus: You can also put lingerie in the box, if she is okay with such a gift. See "How to Buy Lingerie Without Dying of Embarrassment" on page 184.

July 26 Service

Fancy Drinks

With the warm (or hot depending on where you live) weather here, bless her with a cool drink that's just a bit special:

- Learn to make fresh lemonade or limeade.
- Make some frozen drinks in the blender with ice and fruit.
- Get some glass mugs and keep them in the freezer for serving root beer.
- Buy some tiny umbrellas or twisty straws to liven up a plain soda.

July 27 Touch

Go ahead; touch me.

If you aren't "into" touch, you may respond to her touch in a way that communicates to her that you don't want to be touched. Thing is, most women have not only a need to be touched, but to touch those they love.

For her sake, learn to accept her touch as a gift of love. Let her know she is free to touch you when and how she wants.

July 28 Time

Spend your time wisely.

Is there something you spend so much time on that your wife feels cheated? We once had a wife cry, "He loves his bass boat more than he loves me." Her husband spent so much time involved in fishing, and with his fishing buddies, that his wife was jealous – and perhaps rightly so.

We only have so much time, and any time we

spend away from our family is time we can't spend with them. When you were single, your time was your own, but when you married, your time was no longer yours alone.

This is not to say it's wrong to do things away from your wife, but think about what you do and how much time you spend on various activities. Maybe you need to spend a bit less time on some things, and invest the "saved time" in your marriage.

July 29 Prayer

Let Her Know

Let her know you are praying for her. Call her up, or whisper in her ear, "I'm praying for you." Leave a message on the phone, send her an e-mail saying that you are praying for her, or put a "praying for you" sticky note where she will find it.

July 30 Words/Romance

Very Free Verse

For some reason, expressing your love in poetry makes it extra special to her (and no, I don't know why). If you're not poetically gifted, fear not, the effort counts for more than the style. So write a sonnet, a haiku, some free verse, or even a limerick, that expresses your heart for her.

Hint: Bonus points if it's hand written on fancy paper or framed.

July 31 Sex

Sex for Dessert?

Add some fun and flavour to your love making with things you can apply to each other and remove by licking. This is not just for oral sex; it can be fun on many parts of the body as a form of foreplay. You want something that is easy to apply, and won't run. If it's sticky that's great, it takes more tongue action to remove it! Some like the sensation of something cold being applied, while others do not. Warm things as needed by placing in a container of warm water – don't microwave, part of a thick liquid may get hotter than you think.

Barring a food allergy, anything you can eat should be safe to put on your bodies. Things that are spicy hot could be a problem, especially on sensitive skin. Avoid getting things into the vagina, but on the vulva is fine.

A few "topping" ideas:

- Whip Cream (spray can)
- Honey
- Chocolate Sauce
- Guacamole (not the spicy kind)
- Ice cream toppings (butterscotch works well)
- Cheese in a spray can (for the low-carb folks)

August 01 Communication

Don't just do something – stand there.

We're guys, we fix things, it's what we do – right? There are, however, times when your wife does not want you to fix her problem, she just wants you to listen and hug her. Because of how God made you, you see her telling you about a problem as a cry for help – even if she insists she does not want your help.

I understand your need to help, and I'm not here to tell you not to help. However, before you give her what you think she needs, give her what she really came to you for. Hear her out – not just enough to know what the problem is, listen to all the emotion the situation has stirred up in her. Say something that lets her know you've heard her – not just heard what the problem is, but heard the emotion too. Give her a hug and commiserate with her a bit. Only when this is done should you try to fix the problem.

August 02 Service

A Few Extras

Keep an eye out for little things you can do for her. In particular, look for things that might not be "your job."

For example:

- Rinse the couple of plates in the sink and put them in the dishwasher.
- If there is a basket of clean laundry by the washer, carry it to where it goes.
- Bonus points for putting the laundry up in the right way and place!
- Straighten up a room
- Pick up things the kids have left out – or better yet get them to do it, and make sure that they actually do it.

August 03 Gifts

Light up her life, in a small way.

Buy a small flashlight for her to keep in her purse. The disposable "squeeze light" from Energizer® comes in various colours for about $2 For a bit more, get one of the fancy one's that look like a caterpillar, alligator, lizard, or tiger.

Another option now available is an LED flashlight. Because of the low energy use of clear LED's, these lights will give many, many hours of service on one set of batteries.

August 04 Time

Get Cold and Cranky

Make some homemade ice cream together. If you don't want to work too hard for it, buy an electric ice cream maker and let it do the turning. Mix up the cream together, get it going, and sit and talk or cuddle while it freezes. Make a full batch so you can enjoy some right out of the can (it's like soft serve that way) and save the rest for later.

Hint: Buy some small "single serving size" containers and spoon the soft ice cream into them before putting it in the freezer to harden up.

August 05 Sex

I don't know art, but I like you!

It's time to paint your wife! Get a soft brush – anything large and ending in a point is fine, a Sable

Round #10 or #14 would be great. For paint use any edible oil (plain cooking oil is fine). Make sure the room is warm enough, and warm the oil too. Place your "canvas" face up on a large towel on the bed or floor. Start any place you like, but plan on ending with the breasts and genitals. Use a lot of oil, and mix strokes: soft and firm, fast and slow, straight lines, curves and circles.

When you get to her genitals, start around the edges and slowly work inward. First paint just beyond her pubic hair, then move to the outer labia, then the inner labia, and finally to the clitoris. Get just the right brush action on the clitoris and she will either climax or demand you take some other action to cause an orgasm.

When it's over, and she can move, help her clean up. Remove excess oil with a towel, and then help her shower if needed. If the oil does not come off easily, a little bit of dishwashing soap (the kind for the sink, not the dishwasher) should take care of it. Be careful, the oil will make the shower very slippery.

➢➢ She's worth it! ⮜⮜

August 06 Words

Secret Message Inside

Buy your wife a nice card with a distinctive front. Write a very loving or encouraging note inside the card. After she has opened and read the card, have it framed and hang it on the wall, or set it where she will see it often. Each time she sees the card she will remember the loving words it contains.

August 07 Touch

Get Seamy

Trace all the seams on your wife's clothing with a single finger. Move slowly, starting at her neck and working downward.

August 08 Prayer/Walk

"I'll pray for yours, you pray for mine."

Do you have others who are praying for your marriage? Not because you have some problem you are dealing with, but because prayer is so important. Find a couple you feel is godly, and ask if they will pray for your marriage and "let you" pray for theirs.

Beyond this, make it a point to pray for the marriages of your friends, the people you work with, your neighbors, and the people at church. Take time, as a couple, to ask the Lord to bless others' marriages.

Tip: Be sure and put your pastor and church leaders at the top of the list of marriages for which you are praying!

August 09 Service

The sixth Saturday of next month – I promise.

Do you expect "credit" for an act of service that is done days or weeks after it was supposed to be done? Do you think she should be impressed you just did something she asked you to do last month?

Don't make promises you can't or won't keep,

keep the promises you do make, and do everything you can to be timely.

August 10 Gifts/Time

Box Dinner

Give her a nicely wrapped box containing an after dinner mint and a card that invites her to dinner and ________.

August 11 Sex

Necking

Have you ever tried nuzzling, nibbling or gently biting the side of your wife's neck? There's a good chance this will have an arousing effect on her. If this is something new, start with some kissing and see how she responds. Gradually intensify the action over a few days or weeks until you find the perfect intensity for her maximum enjoyment.

Bonus: If she really likes this, she may enjoy having you do the same to her breasts – just be a lot gentler!

August 12 Words

What does it mean?

What do you mean when you say, "I love you" to your wife? What does she mean when she says it to you? Sometimes it means, "I'm sure glad I married you and not someone else." Sometimes it means, "I really enjoy your sense of humor." Sometimes it means, "Let's get naked." Sometimes it means, "You are my best friend."

Try replacing "I love you" with what the words mean at that moment. Get your wife to do the same. Do it for a few days, and see what you learn about each other.

August 13 Gifts/Romance

Two by Two

Every time you and your wife celebrate a special occasion (anniversary, birthday, birth of a child, special trip together), buy a pair of glasses to toast the occasion (you can use wine, non-alcoholic wine, grape juice, milk or Pepsi One® as you like). Save the glasses and display them where you will see them regularly. What kind of glasses does not matter – from leaded crystal goblets to bright pink plastic tumblers, get what seems right to the two of you for each occasion.

August 14 Time

First Day of School Luncheon

If you have kids in public or private school, arrange to make their first day back at school a special day for your wife. At the very least, take off enough time to take her to lunch. If you can swing it, take the day off and hang out with her – go to a matinee movie, have lunch, go window-shopping, whatever. If you have one or more children not yet in school, try to arrange some baby-sitting.

Hot Tip: Be sure to get back to the house at least an hour before the kids will be home!

August 15 Service

A Candle and a Screwdriver

Do you have any drawers that don't open easily? If it has no wheels or bearings, you can make it move much more freely by rubbing the wooden runners with a candle. For drawers with fancy hardware, tightening a screw or two can fix them right up. If screws are missing or won't tighten, get a screw just a bit larger to replace it.

August 16 Sex

Kiss, kiss, kiss, kiss, kiss, kiss...

Lay her naked body on the bed, face down, and slowly kiss from her feet to her head. Pay a lot of attention to the backs of the knees, the small of the back, and the neck. When you get to the top, have her roll over, and kiss her from head to toe.

Hint: It's okay if you never get back down to her feet!

August 17 Touch

Getting to the Bottom...

Give her rear a good rub! The "derriere" has many nerve endings, and because it's a large muscle, it can take a good firm massage. Nudity is optional – the next time you catch her laying around with her backside up, give it a good massage right through her clothes.

August 18 Time

Strategic Retreat

Have you ever been to a marriage seminar or retreat with your wife? Maybe it's time to try one. Since fall is when many such events are offered, now is a good time to plan. There are groups all over the world that offer various Christian marriage weekends, so you should be able to find something near you in a flavour that you will like.

Hint: To find seminars, try putting the following in an Internet search engine: Christian "marriage seminar"

August 19 Prayer

God, make me a better husband!

Pick some aspect of husbanding and start praying about it. Ask the Lord to show you what you should be doing, and to make you aware of your failures in this area. After a few days of prayer, ask your wife to tell you, honestly and bluntly, how you are doing in this area. If she holds back, ask again; tell her you are trying to change and need her to be honest so you can work on it. Then pray some more. Things you could pray about (when you get one right, pick another):

- Being home from work on time
- Being patient with her and the kids
- Being sensitive to her mood
- Being sensitive to her needs
- Being more romantic
- Being a better lover
- Being more financially wise
- Being better about taking care of things she needs you to do around the home.

(I'd go on, but I already feel convicted!)

August 20 Words

Hubba Hubba!

Compliment your wife on her looks. Don't make things up or exaggerate, just honestly tell her something about the way she looks that you really like.

Hot Bonus: Do the same about some sexual part of her anatomy.

August 21 Service

Nice and Neat

Do you have CDs, videos, DVDs, or cassette tapes in abundance? Go buy storage racks to make them nice and neat.

Hint 1: Slim line cases cut CD and DVD storage space in half.
Hint 2: The best way to organize 8-tracks is in the trash!

August 22 Sex

Watching the Clock

A new position to try – this one has received rave reviews from many folks on our on-line forum, so don't knock it until you try it!

Imagine a clock face on the bed to help "see" how to do this. Your wife lies on her back with her head at 12 o'clock and her feet at 6 o'clock. Her knees are bent and her feet are flat on the bed so her legs form an upside down "V." You are on your right side under her legs with your feet at 9 o'clock and head at 3 o'clock; your body be lifting her feet off the bed a bit. Wiggle around until you archive penetration – it's easiest if she guides you in. You will need to lean forward a bit to get the angle right. Once you're together, have her move her right leg between your legs while her left leg stays over your left hip. To help you move better you can grab the top edge of the mattress with your right hand and her right leg with your left hand. Unless you have a too much tummy or she is pregnant, this is an easy and restful position that you should be able to maintain for an extended time. Penetration is shallow, and vigorous movement is not possible, but since the glans of your penis is in the tighter outer area of the vagina this position can be strongly stimulating for you. Her hands are free, and she can easily reach your testicles. Your left hand can be used to stimulant her breasts or clitoris.

Bonus: A fun thing to try with this position is to lay still and use your hand or a vibrator to bring her to orgasm.

August 23 Walk

Speak Blessing

Use the power of your words to bless your wife. Bless her with life, peace, and health. Start each day by blessing her aloud, and go to sleep each night having blessed her again.

August 24 Touch

I wanna hold your haa-aaa-aand...

It's so simple we forget it – holding hands; do it while you walk, sitting together on the couch, or at a movie. Take her hand when you kiss her hello or goodbye. Hold her hand when she is talking to you. Make a point of holding hands with her regularly.

➢➢ **I've said it before, I'll say** ⮜⮜
➢➢ **it again - she's worth it!** ⮜⮜

August 25 Holiday/Gifts

Count Down

Hey guys, it's four months until Christmas – time to start looking for those special little things to give her. Not the "big gift" (if you do that) but the small things you put in her stocking, leave on her pillow, or hide all over the place. If you keep your eyes open and start now, you should have a number of nice and unique things by the time you need them.

August 26 Words

Strong Medicine

Save an empty pill bottle and fill it with small slips of paper on which you have written loving things. If you want to get fancy, replace the bottle's label with a custom label giving contents, suggested dosage, side effects, and other such things, like "to be taken with chocolate."

"A merry heart does good, like medicine." (Pr 17:22a)

August 27 Sex

Two Views – His and Hers

Learn about her, and let her learn about you, by writing sexual fantasies for each other. The fantasy should be about the two of you, and should not go any place you would not really go. You can each write a fantasy based on the same agreed upon premise, each of you can come up with a premises for the other, or each of you can write two fantasies based on premises each of you suggests.

When you share the fantasies, notice how her focus differs from yours. Use this information to help you understand her sexuality better, and to make sex more interesting, fulfilling, and exciting for her.

August 28 Time

Fall Into a Vacation

It's time to plan a fall trip with your wife. A night's stay away is nice if you can swing it, but even a few hours together on a road trip makes for a nice change.

By the way, if you don't have kids keeping you home during the week, you can get great rates now that the kids are back in school and family trips are limited to the weekends.

➢➢ Praise her. ⮜⮜

"Many daughters have done well, But you excel them all. Charm is deceitful and beauty is passing, But a woman who fears the Lord, she shall be praised. Give her of the fruit of her hands, And let her own works praise her in the gates." Proverbs 31:29-31

➢➢ ⮜⮜

August 29 Service

Little Things that Mean a Lot

Try to find some "little things" you can do to make her life easier, or at least less frustrating.

Some little things:

- ➢ Turn you socks right side out when you remove them.
- ➢ Don't put empty or 99% empty containers back in the fridge or cabinet.
- ➢ Replace the toilet paper roll when you finish it. (Note that two sheets left do not count as a roll!)
- ➢ Move the car seat back after you drive.
- ➢ Put the toilet seat up – and back down!
- ➢ Remove your dishes from the table.
- ➢ **Teach your kids do these things too**.

August 30 Touch

Cheat if you have to!

Play a game, with the winner getting a massage from the loser. **Make sure you lose!**

August 31 Gifts

When in doubt, give money!

Give your wife some money to spend on herself, but don't just hand her cash. Using quarters or dollar bills spell out "I love you," or make a big heart.

September 01 Sex/Communication

Oooh, Aaaah

During sex, does she know when she does something you really like? Chances are your body language is not as clear to her as you think it is, so speak up. An occasional "yes," or "oh baby," or a good moan will help her know she is pleasing you and might get her to repeat the things that really feel good. Maybe she will follow your example and start to give you a better indication of what you do that she really likes.

September 02 Words

"You did well not killing that person!"

When you see your wife deal well with a difficult person, be sure to compliment her afterwards.

If this is an area where she is trying to improve, let her know when you see improvement, even if she still failed to act the way she would like to.

September 03 Walk/Holiday

Rosh Hashanah, the Jewish "New Year," happens sometime during the next month. It is tempting for us to think, "I'm not Jewish, I don't need to know about that" – but the roots of Christianity are deeply planted in Judaism. Most of the Bible, including the New Testament, was written by Jews or Jewish believers. Jesus was a Jew, He spoke to Jews, and His words made frequent reference to Jewish tradition; those who do not know this tradition miss much of the depth and richness of what Jesus said.

Therefore, if you want to know Jesus better, and want to understand the truth of the Bible more fully, I recommend learning about our Jewish roots. Do a bit of study on Rosh Hashanah as a starting place, and go from there.

Like Easter, Rosh Hashanah is not celebrated on a fixed day. The holiday begins at sunset (the start of the Jewish day) on following dates:
10/03/05, 09/22/07, 09/12/08, 09/18/09, 09/08/10, 09/28/11, 09/16/12, 09/04/13, 09/24/14, 09/13/15

September 04 Gifts

Mum's the Word

Fall mums are now available. The fabulous display you get from a mum makes it a great gift, and in many locations you can plant it outside when the flowers are finished.

Brown Thumb Tips: Look for a plant that is only buds for a month of colour. If the pot has a foil or plastic cover, make a slit in the bottom and place on a plate to prevent over watering.

September 05 Service

How do you serve me, let me count the ways...

If acts of service are important to your wife, she probably does many acts of service for you; we tend to give that which we want to receive, and we like to know that what we give is appreciated. Pay attention, and make sure to thank her for the things she does for you.

September 06 Time

Just don't send a ransom note.

Why not kidnap your wife? It can be for lunch, for the afternoon, for the day, or for a long weekend. Make sure you have covered everything, including notifying anyone who was expecting her to be some place or do something while you have her in custody.

You can probably get her girlfriends to help out, as they will think it's "just so sweet." Get one of them to make fake plans with your wife so you can ensure she will be free to be taken away, or use one of them to get her away from the house when you need to pack, or to get her to the location where you plan to "abduct" her.

September 07 Sex

Double Sixes!!

Ever wish you had a "safe" way of knowing how interested or not interested she is in sex? Wish you could let her know how interested you are without having to bring it up? Get a pair of dice, the bigger the better, (the fuzzy dice at auto stores are perfect) and place them in the bedroom or bathroom. You each get a die, which you use to indicate your current level of sexual desire by which number is facing up.

Make up your own scale, or use the one below:
1 = No interest, but I'd do if you really need to.
2 = No interest, but not really opposed to it either.
3 = Mildly aware and interested – it could be nice....
4 = I'm ready if you are.
5 = If not today, then tomorrow for sure.
6 = I need you TONIGHT!!

September 08 Words

The Final Word

What's the last thing she hears from you at night? "I love you" is a great choice, while "did you iron my shirt" is a very bad one. Be aware.

September 09 Touch

Your bath is ready.

Give her a first rate bath. Buy some bath salts or bubble bath and run a bath for her. Set a few "smell good" candles around for light. When she gets in, take her towel and toss it in the dryer. Give her back a good washing for her, then sit near by and talk with her while she soaks. When she's done, get the warm towel, wrap her up in it, and give her a long hug.

September 10 Gifts/Romance

Like a High School Student

Do the stores around you sell corsages for the high school homecoming game? High school boys who want to impress their gal buy her a fancy corsage with streamers, glitter, and tokens. The girls wear them like a badge of honour.

If this is a custom in your town, why not buy a corsage for your wife, to show her your love? Alternatively, think of some other gift giving custom that's in style now, or was when you were younger, and give her one of whatever.

September 11 Walk/Prayer

What if you lost her?

For those in the USofA this date will be one of remembrance for many years to come. On this date, in 2001, hundreds of men and women suddenly lost their spouse. As you say a prayer for those individuals, think about what your life would be like without your wife. Would the argument you had last week matter if she suddenly died? Would that annoying little habit of hers matter if she were gone?

It's human nature to take things for granted

until it's too late. Don't take your wife for granted, and make sure she knows you don't.

September 12 Service

Now is a good time for an act of service.

How often does your wife ask you to do some little thing, and you say "later" or put if off for no good reason? Maybe you don't want to interrupt what you're doing, maybe saying "later" is a passive/aggressive control thing, or maybe it's something else. Whatever the reason, think of the blessing it would be to her if you got into the habit of immediately doing what she requested of you. I'm not suggesting you should never say later, but if you are like many men, you could say later a lot less often. Isn't she worth it?

➢➢ *"So husbands ought to love their own* ⋞⋞
➢➢ *wives as their own bodies; he who* ⋞⋞
➢➢ *loves his wife loves himself."* Eph 5:28 ⋞⋞

September 13 Sex

Place Settings for Two

Ever tried sex on the table? She sits on the edge of the table, and then lies back. You support her legs as you stand between them. She inserts you, and away you go.

If she enjoys receiving oral sex, start with her in the same position and you in a chair in front of her. After she is fully satisfied, you can stand up and have intercourse.

September 14 Words

Be a mirror for her.

We all have a hard time knowing how we come across to others and most of us under estimate how much, and how often, we bless others. Watch your wife, and look for times when her words or actions have blessed someone else. Then, when you're alone with her, tell her what you saw by saying something like, "You really blessed Jill when you..."

➢➢ **She's worth it!** ➣➣

September 15 Time

Find out, and then do it again!

Ask your wife some questions that will give you insight you can use to bless her in the future:

For example:
- ➢ What's the nicest thing I've ever done for you?
- ➢ What's the best surprise I've given you?
- ➢ What little things do I do that bless you?
- ➢ What have I stopped doing that you really miss?

September 16 Gifts

Almost like cash, but better.

If she has a bad habit of spending what you give her on others, give a gift certificate to some place that she likes. A bed and bath shop, a bookstore, even a fast food place she likes.

September 17 Service

Small Repairs and Replacements

Save her some work by repairing or replacing something for her.

- Shower curtain growing new life forms? Get a new one and hang it for her.
- Some regularly used item broken or held together with duct tape? Replace it.
- Cabinet door that won't stay closed? Buy an inexpensive magnetic catch and install it for her.

September 18 Touch

Hands on Touch

Ever given your wife a hand massage? Spend several minutes on each hand, stroking gently, firmly but carefully rubbing the muscles, and sliding your hand down her fingers. You can get away with this surprisingly intimate act just about anywhere. Try it at dinner (at home or out) or while waiting for a movie, a concert, or a game. This is also great when you are watching TV together or lying in bed.

September 19 Sex

Godly girls do!!!

Have you affirmed your wife's God given sexuality recently? There are so many competing and confusing messages about sex these days, and this can seriously wound a woman. Maybe she's been taught, "only bad girls enjoy sex" or "only whores do that." Let her know that you thank God for making her a sexual woman, and release her into the freedom she has in Christ to explore and fully enjoy that sexuality.

September 20 Words

Hubby say...

Go to the grocery store and look for a bag of fortune cookies in the "ethnic foods aisle." With a pair of tweezers, carefully exact the "fortunes" inside (you may have to tear the paper and pull half out from each side). Next print up your own special messages, and re-stuff the cookies. Give her one for dinner each night, hide where she will find them during the day, or leave on her pillow when she is in the shower.

September 21 Service

The ultimate stain fighter – YOU!

Do you notice stains on household items? Never mind, does your wife? There are some good stain removing products out there now (and some junk too, buyer beware), so do a bit of research, head down to the HomeDepot® or other "home center," and see if you can make a few things around the house look nicer.

Bonus: While you're at it, think about the scratches on wood items – there are some great and easy fillers and stains.

September 22 Walk

Berean Snack

The next time you have a special speaker at church, take your wife out for coffee or dessert afterwards. Use the time together to discuss what you have heard, if you think it's scriptural, and how you might apply it to your lives.

September 23 Time

A Special Penny for My Thoughts

Find a distinctive penny; it could be from the year you were born, or a foreign penny, or one of those flattened/stamped pennies you can make in the machines found at tourist locations. Give the penny to your wife, and tell her that whenever she hands that penny to you, you will tell her what is going on in your mind at that moment. And yes, you have to give it back to her so she can use it again.

September 24 Gifts

Replacement Gifts

Be on the look out for things she uses that are getting worn out – and buy her a new one. Maybe her umbrella or slippers are old. Maybe a favourite kind of pen is about out of ink, or her pad of sticky notes is about empty. It could even be the scrubber sponge by the sink! The fact that you noticed and took the effort to replace an item will mean a lot to her. Hey, it's not every woman who finds a scrubber sponge with a bow on it by her sink!

September 25 Sex

Honour Bound

Try tying each other up – not with ropes, but with your promise. Place her hands and/or feet where you want them, and tell her she is bound by her honour not to move them; or have her do the same to you. This game does not have the fear factor or negative connotation of "bondage" and it's easy to "untie" your partner at a moments notice.

September 26 Service

Hide it in a box under the bed instead.

Do you have a "junk drawer"? Is it so full that pulling it out means spending several minutes rearranging it so it will close again? Does it drive your wife crazy?

Dump everything into a box and sort through it while watching your favourite sport. If you can't throw anything out (you know you will need it the day after the trash is collected) at least find another home for some of the less often needed items.

September 27 Touch

Play

As kids, we did a lot of playing that involved touching. We tickled, we wrestled, and we played tag. Try adding some playful touch to your relationship – a pillow fight, a wrestling match, thumb wrestling, whatever.

September 28 Words

Random acts of sticky notes and sensible encouragement.

Buy some small sticky notes, in various colours, and go on an encouraging-words-on-sticky-notes rampage. Scatter them all over, or apply heavily in one small area. Put them on cans and boxes in the pantry, plaster the bathroom, put them in her purse, do the ceilings. Do the inside of cupboard doors, the wall under the showerhead, the rear view mirror of the car, or the TV. Have fun blessing her!

Tip: Surprise her for days by stashing notes where she will not immediately find them: a plate half way down a stack of plates, a towel in the middle of a stack, or unroll some of the toilet paper roll, stick a note on, then roll it back up.

September 29 Sex/Communication

Dear Sex Diary...

Keep a sex diary in a book or on your computer, and give your wife free access to it. Write in the diary each time you have sex – not just what happened, but how you felt about it. Make note of things you really liked as well as things you didn't. Mention when you think she liked something, and when you think she didn't. Also, mention your disappointment about things that didn't happen.

I know it's scary being that open about your sexual feelings and thoughts; but as your wife reads, she will learn a lot about you, and what would make sex better for you. She may also learn about mistakes in what you think she feels, wants, and would or would not do. A sex diary could improve your sexual communication, and that would bless both of you.

September 30 Gifts

Beat up on this gift!

If your wife has a really bad day (or week, or month), get her a piñata and let her take her aggressions out on it.

Hint: If she is a chocoholic, try to find a piñata full of chocolate candy.

October 01 Time

Fall Drive

Fall is here and it's beautiful out. Take a drive out in the country, find somewhere to park, and take a walk together. Pack something cold or hot to drink, and a small snack.

October 02 Service/Romance

Open and Shut

How long has it been since you held a door for your wife, or opened and shut the car door for her? How about pulling out her chair or helping her with her coat? All these things were common a half a century ago, before feminists made it down right unsafe to do them. The truth is these acts were not an insult or put down; they were a sign of respect and love. Try it; she might like it!

October 03 Sex

Get her to kiss and tell.

Ask your wife to share with you one of the most memorable sexual experiences she's ever had with you. Listen to what it was that made it so nice for her; it may not be what you would expect. Use this little glimpse into her mind to help make your lovemaking better in the future.

October 04 Words

You look marvelous, darling.

Do you say nice things about the way she looks? She needs to hear from you that you like the way she looks, the way she dresses, the way she does her hair. Make a point of really looking at her so you will know when she has a new hairdo or new dress.

And no, I don't know a safe answer to, "Does this make me look fat?"

October 05 Touch

Spa for One

Have you ever wondered why folks will spend a fortune to go to a spa? Sure, it's relaxing, and it's nice to be waited on hand and foot, but I think one of the biggest reasons spas are so popular is that it gives people a chance to receive touch. If you want to give your wife that kind of touch, get a few things from the health and beauty section of the grocery store or pharmacy and give her a mini spa at home.

Start with a nice bath. Add bath salts, bubble bath, or effervescent bath tablets. Or go all out and buy one of those "turn-your-tub-into-a-whirlpool" devices that sits over the side of the tub and shoots out bubbles and jets of water. While she's soaking, offer a nice cold glass of her favourite beverage. Next, move to the bed, or some other place she can comfortably lay down. Cover her with a towel to keep her warm, and apply a facial mask. Massage lotion into her feet while the mask is on, and then remove the mask.

Finish up with an all over massage, using a body lotion. Finally, lie down and snuggle with her until she nods off, gets up, or jumps you!

October 06 Time

1 book 4 2

Read a book together. I do mean **together** – curl up together, and one of you read out loud. The book can be whatever you both like – a mystery, non-fiction, Christian, self-help, history, or humorous. Set aside some time each day, or a couple of days a week, to read.

October 07 Sex

Sex Games

Play some short easy game (tic-tac-toe, hangman, blackjack). The winner of each round gets to take off one piece of the other's clothing. If the opponent is naked, then the winner gets to spend one minute doing whatever they like. Keep playing until you both win by "losing it" and having sex.

October 08 Words

You are the second best thing that ever happened to me.

Make a list of all the ways you are a better man because of her, and leave it where she can't miss it.

➢➢ **She's worth it!** ⋞⋞

October 09 Service

When eating out could save your life...

Picture this: your lovely wife has had a really long day, she's stressed out of her mind, and when she goes to make dinner one of the ingredients she needs is not to be found, or she can't get the stove to work, or just looking at the sink makes her whimper.

At this point eating out is all but a medical emergency for her. If you know a ladle from a skillet you could do the cooking, but that does not give her the mental break she really needs. Depending on what's best for her either take everyone out or go and bring dinner in.

Hint: If you're on a tight budget, you need to plan ahead for this: put aside a few dollars at a time for an emergency meal situation.

October 10 Touch

Back-words Spelling

When she's lying on her front side, and her back is naked, use your finger to spell "I LOVE YOU" on her back in big letters. Keep doing it, slowly, until she catches on.

October 11 Prayer

Pray for a Full Fruit Wife

Pray for God's will for your wife to be manifested more and more in her life. Also, pray that you will not do anything that might hamper God's will, and that God can use you to help His will for your wife to come to full fruit.

October 12 Gifts/Romance

Money That Talks

Give her some cash, but not just any old cash. Get some nice new bills, and write messages of love on each one. A fine point red marker on the top margin of the bill works well. Keep the messages G rated, and have fun telling her you love her.

Legal point: No, this is not illegal, at least not in the USofA. Title 18, Section 333 of the United States Code only prohibits "defacement of currency in such a way that it is made unfit for circulation." Therefore, small writing in the margins is legal.

October 13 Sex

Gee!

Inside the vagina is a spot called, among other things, the G-spot. The G-spot has been called "her other hot button" because stimulation can be very enjoyable. This spot is an inch or two in, on the upper side. You can reach the G-spot by inserting one or two fingers into her vagina, palm facing up. At first, you may not feel anything, but if you gently rub or make a "come hither" motion with your fingers, the area should become firmer than the surrounding tissue.

Initially stimulation of the G-spot may cause her to feel a need to urinate. This feeling will pass, and may be replaced by pleasure. Responses to stimulation of the G-spot vary widely; some women can have an orgasm from this stimulation alone, while others find stimulation of only the G-spot to be too little to arouse them, or even mildly uncomfortable. Women generally enjoy G-spot stimulation more if they are already well aroused when it begins, and most women will enjoy it as an addition to stimulation of the clitoris.

October 14 Time

Movie Night

Rent a video or two, make some popcorn, and snuggle up together with the lights off. Enjoy the movie, and being together.

Hot Hint: Making out is encouraged!

October 15 Words

Secret Sign of Encouragement

Is there something your wife faces about which she feels uncomfortable or unsure? Maybe she is nervous around strangers, has a hard time accepting compliments, or is uncomfortable speaking in a group. Create a nonverbal signal that means, "You can do it" or "You were great" or "Hang in there." The signal can be something like scratching your ear with your pinky, or folding your hands in a way you don't normally do.

October 16 Service

Is it just me, or is it dark in here?

Are there any burnt out light bulbs in your home? Is that five-bulb fixture down to two bulbs? Make a point of replacing bulbs as soon as they burn out. Even if one or more are bulbs still working in a fixture, change the burnt out one(s).

Tip: The new screw-in florescent bulbs cost more up front, but they last longer and only use about one forth as much electricity for the same amount of light. These bulbs also put out considerably less heat.

October 17 Touch

Flannel Socks Allowed

Cold weather is on the way. Does that mean your lovely wife's bedtime nudity is about to disappear into a flannel cocoon for the next few months? Women run cooler than men for hormonal reasons, so if you want sleep time nudity in the winter you will have to work at it. An electric blanket with dual controls works well, or you can add an extra layer (or two) of blanket on her side of the bed between the sheet and the regular blanket.

If she must dress for bed, try to keep her from covering from head to toe. Be prepared to keep the room a bit warmer. Get her some heavy socks. Find her a long sleeve top and encourage her to go bottomless.

➢➢ Her children will respect her if you do. ≺≺

October 18 Sex/Romance

Thank You!

Leave a note on her pillow thanking her for being such a great lover; or creative lover, or adventurous, or considerate, or willing, or whatever sounds right.

Hint: An unsealed envelope is a nice touch.

October 19 Prayer/Communication

Openly Honest

Pray for openness and honesty in your marriage. Then follow up with actions – if you've done anything to damage openness and honesty in your marriage, repent and ask your wife to forgive you.

October 20 Words

Erasable Encouragement.

Buy a small white board and marker – you can get them the size of a sheet of paper with or without a bit of artwork or a cartoon on them. Post the board in a private place where your wife will see it daily – the back of your bedroom or bathroom door works well. Daily write a love note or other encouragement on the white board.

October 21 Gifts

It's her to a T.

Buy her a T-shirt with a saying that fits her philosophy, or a design that "is her" or a picture of something she loves. (Check her existing T-shirts for size.)

October 22 Sex

Easy Does It

There are times when a woman may want and need to have an orgasm, but will shy away from sex because she is too tired or too stressed. She feels she is not going to be able to get there, or that her husband is not willing to do what it would take, or is just afraid of getting even more worked up only to be left high and dry. This probably does not make a lot of sense to you, because you are a guy. Sex is generally easy for us – much easier than it is for women. Most women say that getting to orgasm "takes some work," even when they are aroused and eager.

If you can grasp the idea, and learn to tell when she may be shying away from sex because of these things, you can help her and bless both of you.

If you are willing to meet her on her terms, and do what she wants, how she wants it, she might let you give her the release she really needs. Set aside your ideas about "how sex is supposed to be," turn off your ego, and serve her. Your only goal at these times should be to give her the orgasm she needs as easily as possible.

October 23 Time

Out of Time Again

It's impossible to have quality time with your wife if you don't have enough time with her. Make some time to sit down with your wife and talk with her about how you use your time, what you could do to use time more efficiently, and how each of you could save time to give each other. You might also want to reevaluate where your time goes, and see if you need to cut back on certain things.

October 24 Service

Get that car winterized!

With winter coming, it's important for the car she uses to be running correctly, and be ready for whatever winter in your area throws at you. Give the car the twice over, or take it to a shop to have it done. Make sure she has what she needs in the car: ice scraper, gloves, flashlight, and a can of "Fix-a-flat."

Bonus: Don't forget her emergency chocolate stash!

October 25 Touch

Slow Dancin'

Put on some appropriate music and do some slow dancing – naked. If it leads to sex that's great, but don't make that the goal it. Just enjoy the feeling of her skin against yours, her head on your shoulder, and so on.

Hint: Disco is dead for a reason!

October 26 Gifts

Flowers That Never Wilt

Get her a framed picture of a nice flower arrangement in a pretty vase. Red roses are good, or look for her favourite flower. From a small stand-alone frame to a poster size photo, it's a flower that won't be in the trash next week.

October 27 Walk/Prayer

Why don't we pray?

When your wife is frustrated, hurt, down, stressed or otherwise not a happy camper, do you ask her if she would like to take a moment to pray with you? Drag her aside and pray for her situation and her general sanity.

Confession: It usually annoys me when my wife does this to me, but I always appreciate it later.

October 28 Sex

Quantity vs. Quality

When it comes to sex, which is more important, quantity or quality? The majority of men will say quantity, while most women will say quality. Neither answer is "right," my point is that this is just one more way in which women's sexual views and needs differ from ours.

A "quickie" may be fine for you, and she may enjoy it or enjoy giving it to you, but she needs a lot more than that for sex to be satisfying for her. She needs your time, and your attention, and your focus on what makes sex good for her. What most women want is more both before and after intercourse: more foreplay, and more before foreplay, and more snuggling, and more murmuring of "I love you" after the "big bang."

October 29 Words

That blessed me.

When she does something that helps or blesses you, make a point of telling her so immediately. You don't have to use fancy words or go on and on, just tell her that her actions have made your day easier, or made you happy, or made you feel loved.

Hot Bonus: If she truly blesses you sexually, go out of your way to tell her so. Many women feel inadequate sexually, and even those who are more than meeting their husband's needs may fear they are falling short.

October 30 Time

See you after the play offs, honey.

Are you a sports fan in a big way? Unless you have one of those rare wives who are really into football/basketball/golf/tennis/baseball/hockey/soccer/wrestling/NASCAR, your devotion to your sport(s) of choice may be a source of frustration for her. If you can give her as much time as you give the sport, she will probably not complain, but if the sport gets more quality time than she does, she has a reason to feel unloved, doesn't she? Spend some time thinking about that balance, then increase the time you spend with her and/or decrease the time spent with sports until she's getting as much of you as your sports are.

Think of it this way, folks on their deathbed have lamented the lack of time they spent with family, but no one says, "I wish I had watched more golf!"

October 31 Service

Secret Acts of Service

How many little things can you do for her without her being aware? Make it a game you play. When she catches you, she will be blessed. When she does not catch you, she will still be blessed – she just won't know it.

November 01 Romance/Gifts

Etched in Stone – or Something

Create a love message that will endure. Carve a heart and your initials in a tree, have them etched on a glass or a mirror (do it yourself kits at your local craft store), or write a few words in concrete that's setting up. Another option – have a picture of the two of you framed with an inscription in calligraphy.

November 02 Touch

Call It in the Air

Give your bride a coin and ask her to flip it. If it lands heads you give her a big kiss, if it lands tails you give her a good hug. Then walk away. Repeat regularly.

Hot Bonus: Think of a different set of results to use in the bedroom!

November 03 Sex

A use for those throw pillows!

It's amazing how much you can change some sex positions simply by putting a pillow under one of you. Extra pillows can also make things like foreplay and oral sex both easier and more enjoyable. So, stop looking sideways at those fancy pillows your wife wants to pile on the bed, and find a way to use them for better sex.

Hint: If the pillow you're using does not have a removable, washable cover, be sure to place a small towel over it.

November 04 Time

You're important; I just don't have time for you.

Have you ever said that to your wife? Probably not in words, but have your actions ever said it to her? No matter how busy you are she needs some alone time with you. When life is busy and time is short, make sure you show her how important she is to you by giving her the time she needs and deserves!

➢➢ **She's worth it!** ≺≺

November 05 Gifts

A Stuffy Gift

Do women ever out grow the love of stuffed animals? Not from what I've seen – I think it's some sort of childhood holdover – receiving a stuffed animal makes a woman feel loved. Get her something stuffed you think she would like, from a giant panda to a Beanie Baby cat.

Hint: If she likes it, buy a whole herd for her. Silently add animals when she's not looking.

November 06 Words

Encouragement in a Jar

Buy a nice little jar, or a fancy box, and fill it with small notes of encouragement on folded pieces of paper. Write about her best traits, her triumphs, her best body parts, and how she blesses you. Leave the jar/box on her dresser where she can read a few notes whenever she feels the need.

Tip: Be sure to sneak in new notes from time to time.

November 07 Service

Where do socks go?

What "little things" do you do that irritate your wife? Well stop it! Often it's the "small stuff" that bothers us the most, and you can greatly bless her by cutting out a few of your more annoying habits. It could be something destructive, like smoking or not exercising, or something trivial, like biting your nails, never getting your socks in the hamper, or saying "you know" every 20 words. Breaking a habit that really bothers her is a major act of service – but she's worth it!

November 08 Prayer

A Timely Prayer

One of the most precious resources we have is time. Our society tends to be excessively busy, and it's a challenge for each of us to use our time wisely.

Pray about and for your wife's time management. It doesn't matter if she's strong or weak in this area, we can all benefit from more wisdom in deciding how to invest our time.

November 09 Romance

I heart you.

Leaving heart shapes for her to find is a simple way to let her know you love her and think about her often. Silly (to you) things like a ketchup heart on her plate, a paper clip bent into the shape of a heart, or a heart drawn in dust on a foggy widow, will warm her heart and make her feel loved.

November 10 Gifts

Get "credit" for practical gifts.

If you've ever given a practical gift at a "designated gift giving time," you probably discovered this is not considered a good thing in her mind. However, giving a practical gift at a "non-designated gift giving time" is considered a good thing.

If you know she has run out of something, anything from milk to cleanser to toilet paper, buy some, put a bow on it, and leave it for her.

November 11 Touch/Sex

Let me oxytocin you, babe.

Science corner: For a woman to want and enjoy sex, she needs to have a good dose of the hormone oxytocin in her system. Any kind of "good touch" raises oxytocin levels, but certain areas of her body trigger more oxytocin release than others. Her neck, lips, and breasts are good, and the nipples are the great; sucking the nipples is particularly effective.

Now you know why these areas of her body are so special to her, and why foreplay is so important. If you want a warm reception when you get "down stairs," be sure to take care of matters "upstairs" first.

Bonus: Keep her oxytocin fires burning all day long with hand and foot rubs, back and shoulder massages, and plenty of hugging and kissing.

November 12 Walk

Accountability

There's a lot of talk of accountability groups or accountability partners in many parts of the church today. This is a very Biblical and needed thing, and can be applied to marriage very nicely. Find a man you trust and respect. Ask him to enter into an agreement with you to pray for each other as husbands and fathers, and to regularly ask each other a list of questions about how well you are doing.

This is not a time for gossip, bragging, or bad mouthing; it's a way of making you more aware of how you are doing as a husband, and what areas you need to work on. Write you own list of questions, with the following as a starting place:

- Have you kissed your wife today?
- Have you told her you love her?

- Have you prayed for her?
- Have you put her needs ahead of everyone else's?
- Have you violated her by having sexual thoughts about another woman?
- Finish with, "Have you been completely honest with me in all your answers?"

Hint: The phone is an easy way to connect for these questions. Set a regular time and be diligent about calling daily.

November 13 Time

I believe we have a table near the kitchen.

Find a place for the kids if you have any at home (switch nights with a friend who has kids) and make your wife a meal for just the two of you. (Cooking ideas for anyone, including those who should not cook, on page 190.)

Set a nice table, dim the lights, and set out candles. Dress up; wear a suit and even a tie. Seat your wife, then serve one course at a time. Eat slowly, and enjoy the time together.

Hot Bonus: If you think she would go for it, strip from the waist down before you bring the dessert from the kitchen.

November 14 Service/Gifts

I got it from my secret source.

Is there something she enjoys that she can't find where you live? It might be a food, a candy, a hobby item, or a beauty product. Track down the treasured item and keep a supply on hand for her.

Mail order is your friend in this pursuit. Additionally, the web is a great way to search for products, and what you're looking for is very likely available from an on-line store.

November 15 Words/Communication

The Truth, the Whole Truth, and no White Lies

It's nice to encourage and lift up, but if we're not believable, our words lose the power to make others feel good. Do you sometimes tell little "white lies" to spare your wife's feelings? Surely, she is aware of at least some of those "embellishments," and they make all your encouragements suspect - are you just telling her what you think she wants to hear?

Be honest, even when your words are not what she would like to hear. Always be loving and kind, but also be honest. An occasional truth that hurts lets her know that your compliments and encouragements are valid and sincere.

November 16 Sex

Pseudocourse: almost the "real thing."

Try this for a little change, or when intercourse isn't possible for some reason, or when you climax before she's done (this can be done with or without an erection).

You lie on your back, legs together. Your wife is above as if you were going to have intercourse with her on top. Your penis is lying on your body pointing toward his chin; underside facing up. She lowers herself so that your penis comes into contact with her vulva, between her outer lips. She then either pushes against you (as if thrusting), or she slides up and down (parallel to the bed) along your penis.

Because this activity results in her clitoris rubbing against the most sensitive part of your penis, it's very pleasurable for both of you, and it's possible for both of you to reach climax. Changing the point of contact and the amount of movement will change the intensity of the stimulation for each of you, making it possible to find a method that brings you to orgasm at about the same time. If you climax first, she should be farther down the shaft; if she climaxes first, she needs to up toward the glans.

November 17 Holiday/Gifts

Make a list, check it more than twice ...

It's not too soon to be thinking about Christmas. Keep an eye out for things she needs and things in which she shows an interest. Put some thought into it now, and shop before December 24!

Note: If you're spending lite on Christmas, you'll need to put even more thought it to what you buy. With a bit of thought, you can show your love and for pennies.

November 18 Touch

The Snuggle Button

Do you have a "snooze button" on your alarm clock? Make it the "snuggle button" instead. Set the alarm 10 minutes earlier and take the extra time to slowly wake up snuggling, tell her how wonderful she is, and start the day with prayer.

November 19 Holiday/Prayer

Holiday Prayers on Behalf of the Busy Wife

As much as we love the holiday season, it's also full of busyness, stress, and aggravation. Make a point of praying daily for your wife this holiday season:

- Pray for her schedule and use of time.
- Pray for her to have energy.
- Pray for her to get the food and sleep she needs.
- Pray that you will be sensitive to her needs and her level of stress.

November 20 Holiday/Time

There must be room for more...

Does your wife decorate for Christmas? Does she do it without you until she gets to something she can't do, or can't do alone? Why not make decorating the house, inside and/or out, a way of spending time together. Talk about and plan what you'll do, shop together for anything you need (buy before Thanksgiving), and do the decorating together.

Bonus: Don't forget to make taking down the decorations and packing them away a joint project too!

November 21 Holiday/Service

Stick up for your wife.

When you get together with family for the holidays, be on the lookout for folks giving your wife a hard time. When you're around your family, stand up to anyone – **including your mother** – who is hassling your wife. Around her family, be sure to support your wife and let it be know how much you love her and what a wonderful wife and mother she is.

November 22 Holiday/Service

Disappearing Act

Note: This tip is for Thanksgiving Day.

If your wife has laboured in the kitchen most of the day to get the feast ready, why don't you take care of cleaning it up? I'm not just talking about clearing the table here! Send your wife to soak in the tub while you put the leftovers in proper containers, pack the containers into the fridge, wash the dishes, and put the dishes up.

Hint: If you're not sure where something goes, leave it out so she doesn't have to play hide and seek next time she needs it.

November 23 Words

Thank you, my wife.

Sit down with paper and pen, or screen and keyboard if you prefer, and write your wife a letter describing all the things about her for which you are thankful. Don't just toss out a few lines off the top of your head - really put some time into thinking about it. Are there things she does all the time that have become invisible to you? Does she do things you know cost her more than a bit of time or energy? What about the things she does for your children? Bless her by showing her that you see her efforts, and thanking her for all she does.

November 24 Gifts/Romance

A Kodak® Moment

Think of a location that has special romantic meaning to her; where you first kissed, where you proposed, or some place you went on your honeymoon trip. Get a nice picture of that place, and have it matted and framed. If you want to go all out, find a "starving artist" who will take a photo and make a painting from it. Check the on-line resources on page 213 for a company that will do such artwork for a fee.

November 25 Sex

S L O W L Y...

Up front, let me tell you this is one of those things that a woman either loves or hates; if it's not going well – bail out! Also, be aware this is not a good thing to do when she is tired, or stressed, or has to get up early the next morning. With those warnings…

Try taking sex very, very slowly, with her being stimulated for a long time before she has an orgasm. Unless you have an unusual degree of both self-control and awareness, you can't do this with intercourse, so use your hands, your mouth, a vibrator, or a combination of the three.

Do all the normal foreplay things; only take more time with each. When you finally get between her legs move her fairly quickly to a high level of arousal, then slow down and settle in for the long haul. Tease and titillate. Take her close, and then let her fall back some. If you think she's confused or concerned, let her know you want to make it very good for her by taking a long time. If (when) she begs you to finish, you have to decide if that is really what she wants, or if she will thank you (afterwards) for holding her off even longer.

If she's into it, and you get it right, it will result in an extremely strong and long orgasm. If she likes it, remember that practice makes perfect.

➢➢ If you bless her in public, ≺≺
➢➢ she will bless you in private! ≺≺

November 26 Prayer

See her as God sees her.

Ask the Lord to show you who He wants your wife to be. Not just a vague direction, but a clear image of who He intends her to be, what He's calling her to do, and how He wants to use her. Then pray for those things. Also, be on the look out for things that may prevent God's will for her life so you can stop or minimize their effects.

November 27 Time

Five-Minute Vacation

When life is so crazy you aren't even sure where you are or what day it is, you can bet your wife is suffering for a bit more of your time. Make a point of "taking her away from it all" even if that means going to the bedroom and locking the door for a five minute shoulder rub.

November 28 Touch

Stroke Massage

This is not a typical massage; it's done with a very light touch. Let your whole hand move over her unclothed body with a bit less pressure than you would use to pet a cat. Follow her curves, muscle groups, and other "topography." Move around in a back and forth manner – focus on one area while occasionally stroking both the "next area" and the "last area." Spend extra time on the face, the buttocks, and if she's comfortable with it, the breasts. You can be sexual or not, but see this as a way to bless her in and of itself; if it leads to sex that's a bonus for both of you.

November 29 Words

What affects women the way a short skirt affects men?

Is someone doing a better job of giving your wife compliments and kind words than you are? For a woman this can create the same problem a man experiences when some woman blatantly flirts with him. Your wife needs more than just knowing you love her, honour her, and appreciate her – she need to hear it regularly! Don't leave her hungry and open to temptation.

And yes, it really is a fair comparison. Women who commit adultery don't report they were tempted by the guy's pecs or buns – it's kindness and courteous attention that start women down the path to infidelity.

November 30 Service

Don't Over Commit

Being too busy is one of the biggest problems most of us face, and it hurts our marriages, our children, and us. Be aware of how much you're doing for those outside the family, and make sure you have plenty of time left for doing things for your wife.

I don't believe God calls us to help others, no matter how important it might be, at the expense of the person to whom we're married. Show your wife she really comes first by putting her first in your time management.

Hint: There is a reason this tip's given at this time of the year!

December 01 Holiday/Walk

He Is!

Perhaps you have heard "Jesus is the reason for the season" so many times it seems trite. What we do or don't do, give or don't give, celebrate or don't celebrate, doesn't matter as long as we remain aware of the ultimate gift that Jesus gave us on the cross. As the head of your household, make sure the truth about Jesus is not lost as your family celebrates His birth.

December 02 Sex

"Mirror, mirror..."

Mirrors for sex may seem like a "guy thing" since we men are more easily aroused by what we see than our wives. However, many women enjoy the view offered by a bedside mirror. Some women have told us that "seeing themselves in action" helped them accept their sexual side. Other women are aroused by the sight of their husband being sexual with them.

If you want to try this, start with a mirror on a chair placed beside the bed, and see how she likes it. She might like it as a once in a while thing, or you might both like it so much you'll decide to get something larger and more permanent.

If you want something permanent: mirror tiles are inexpensive and easy to apply, you could move the bed near the closet and install sliding mirrored closet doors, or look for a large standing mirror that can be moved to give varying views.

December 03 Words

It's Tradition!

We can be pretty wrapped up in our traditions, to the point of feeling attacked if our traditions are questioned or treated as unimportant. With this in mind, encourage your wife by encouraging her to practice the holiday traditions of her family. Also, work to create new traditions for your family.

December 04 Time

15 minutes of, ah, fame?

Give her fifteen minutes to ask you anything she wants, and promise to share your mind and your feelings about whatever she asks. Make a habit of doing this – you may never understand how much it means to her, but I assure you it will be a great blessing.

December 05 Holiday

All Wrapped Up

It's time to get serious about those Christmas gifts. The next few days' tips will suggest gift ideas suitable for the various categories discussed throughout this book. Today – Gift Wrap.

In case you didn't get the memo, women do not generally see string, wire, duct tape, or old newspaper as valid gift wrap materials. If you never developed gift-wrapping skills, find other ways to make gifts look nice. Gift bags are great, just add a bit of tissue paper, tie a gift tag on the handle, and you're set! Alternatively, you can find printed gift boxes that look like wrapping paper – just add a stick-on bow. You can also make the wrapping part of the gift with a fancy box, bowl, or other container.

If all else fails, you can get someone else to wrap it for you. Most malls have a wrapping station, and many individual stores do as well. Another option is to take all your gifts to a Mail Box Etc® or Postal Annex®. For a modest fee, they will be happy to do it even if you don't have them mail the packages.

December 06 Gifts –Gifts

Just how much does a pear tree cost?

If your wife is a gifts kind of person, consider doing the twelve days of Christmas thing – give her one gift on the first day, two on the second, and so on for twelve days. The gifts need not be expensive, especially if you are clever about what you give.

Ideas: For day four, you could get a candy sampler that has four pieces of candy. Other good items are candles, bookmarks, nice pens, a set of felt tip markers (an eight marker set on day eight), nail polish, hair barrettes, sexy panties, coasters, drinking glasses, throw pillows, music CDs, and paperback books. You can also "cheat" by getting several low dollar gift certificates for one day.

The traditional twelve days of Christmas starts on Christmas day and runs into the New Year. If you think your wife would enjoy this more after Christmas, or you don't think you can get it all ready by the 14th, go with the "original."

Hint: This tip was requested (demanded?) by several of the ladies on our mailing list a couple of years back. I'd take that as a strong vote of confidence for the idea.

December 07 Gifts – Romance

Twinkle, Twinkle, Little Lights

Sometime shortly before Christmas, take a drive to look at some Christmas light displays. Maybe a town display like a "trail of lights" or a neighborhood where everyone tries to outdo each other. Some newspapers write articles on the best neighborhoods, or you can scout it out before hand. Some Christmas music on the car radio or CD/cassette player adds to the experience, but keep the volume low enough to share your delight with the lights.

Hint: Bring a Thermos of hot chocolate or coffee.

December 08 Gifts – Service

This coupon good for...

Give her coupons good for various tasks you procrastinate about doing, or things she normally does that you could do for her. Be serious about doing what the coupon says when she presents it to you; offer a 2 for 1 deal if you say no when asked.

Throw in a few things like "5 kisses and a bear hug" for fun. Things like "dinner out" are always appreciated, but make it mostly about acts of service you can do for her.

December 09 Gifts – Touch

Go ahead, rub it in!

Buy (or make) a bottle of massage oil and give it to her as a gift. Of course the real gift is using the oil on her – from a quick back rub to a full body massage, each application will bless her. Be on the look out for good times to massage her; physical pain, stress, and tiredness can all be reduced with massage.

Home Made Massage Oil: Any edible oil will work; I like the "feel" of 40 % walnut oil and 60% safflower oil. You can play with the mix ratio; some oils have more "drag" then others. Add a small amount of scented oil; I use peppermint essential oil (not extract) which has a slight warming effect on the skin. A variety of essential oils are available in many drug stores and grocery stores. Always test the mixed oil to make sure there's no allergic reaction. Store oil in the fridge, and float a small squeeze bottle of oil in hot water to warm it for use.

December 10 Gifts – Words/Communication

Write to the Heart.

Give your wife a gift she'll cherish for years to come. Sit down and write her a letter telling her how wonderful she is, how she blesses you, how much you need her, and how much you depend on her. The letter need not be particularly long, but it should be more than a couple of short paragraphs. Put some time into it; think about it, write it, and rewrite it.

Once you have the letter composed, create a nice looking document. Handwritten is a nice touch if your handwriting is legible. If you use a computer, choose a fancy, but readable font. A nice heavy weight paper with a pale pattern or picture is another good touch. Seal it up in an envelope, put her name on it, and leave it where she will find it when she will have a bit of private time to read.

December 11 Gifts – Walk

Give in His Name

What gift are you giving Jesus this year? Talk with your wife (and your children if you have any at home) about doing something to give to others. It can be money, but a gift of labour is even better. Find a needy family, maybe a family in your church who's fallen on hard times, and give them a Christmas they would otherwise not have. Be generous; be very generous.

December 12 Gifts – Time

Time Out

Life getting crazy as Christmas approaches? Having less and less time to spend with your wife? Make a firm date to go out to eat together. When and where are not important, just find a way to make it happen before Christmas.

You may have to be creative to find a time that works for both of you. Can you take a long lunch one day, or maybe go for breakfast on Saturday or Sunday? You may also need to work at child care; find a friend to keep yours a couple of hours in return for you watching theirs, or tap into the out of school baby sitter pool during daylight hours when they are more likely to be available.

Bonus: If you enjoy going to movies together, and you can get your shopping all done before the 24th, the theaters are all but empty on the afternoon of Christmas Eve. Maybe you can make a movie together on that afternoon a new tradition.

December 13 Gifts – Sex

For a very good girl!

Get your wife a private Christmas stocking and put it on her pillow Christmas Eve or Christmas night. What you put in the stocking depends on what she can handle. Perfume, lotion, emery boards, and slipper socks are pretty safe for everyone. If she will be blessed by it, spice things up with some sexy lingerie, flavored oils, or other sexual gifts.

Bonus: See if you can find or make a stocking that is classy, sensuous, or down right sexy; black velvet with her name in gold glitter for example!

➢➢ *Who can find a virtuous wife?* ⋞⋞
➢➢ *For her worth is far above rubies.* ⋞⋞
➢➢ Pr 31:10 ⋞⋞

December 14 Gifts – Romance/Touch

Y'all Texuns is weird.

Here in Texas a friend of our hangs a decorative chili pepper ornament in a doorway each year. My wife and I decided to kiss under it, as if it were mistletoe. Find your own "kissing ornament, hang it where your wife will be under it regularly, and have fun.

December 15 Holiday/Service

Shopping with, for, and without the kids.

There are a number ways you can bless your wife if you have kids at home:

- Help the kids do their shopping for their friends, and for their mom, so your wife does not have to take them.
- Help your wife shop for the kids – go shopping with her if you can, or stop and pick up any large/heavy gifts that are needed.
- If your children are young, offer to take care of them so your wife can go shopping without them.
- Since the weekends are crazy it would be a special blessing if you could take off half a day of work so she does not have to fight as much of a crowd.

December 16 Prayer

Pray for me, woman!

Do you value your wife's prayers? You should! Let her know you want her prayers, and help her out by telling her what prayers you most need.

December 17 Sex

Honey, you are so ... zzzzzzz

Think "after glow" is something made up by women to confuse men? Sorry, it looks like it was God's idea. Sex releases a number of chemicals into our bodies and brains, and those chemicals make women feel very warm, open, and vulnerable. The same chemicals may cause a man to feel so relaxed he drifts off to sleep, which is not what a woman feeling warm, open, and vulnerable wants! Before you snore, snuggle up close and tell her how special she is, and how blessed you are that she's your wife.

December 18 Words/Romance

Advent of a Special Calendar

This will take a bit of time, which is why it's located well before the New Year. Buy a calendar and a bunch of Post-It® notes. Write something nice on each day of the calendar (I love you, you bless me, you make great stew, you have cute buns), then cover them all up with the Post-It's (cut to size as needed). You could also do this with a desk calendar, or you could use a computer to make and print out the calendar pages with the messages already on them.

Present the gift to your wife on New Year's Day, or hang it where she will see it. If your notes are at all personal be sure to hang it where others won't see it, like the inside of your bedroom door.

December 19 Service

Before the Big Dinner

One of the Byerly family traditions is chicken tortilla soup on Christmas Eve, fixed by the man of the house. It's easy, and just about everyone likes it. Check out the recipe in the food section on page 190, and consider taking care of Christmas Eve dinner this year. It will be one less thing your wife has to take care of – what a blessing.

Hint: Make a double batch and save the rest for when everyone is tired of turkey or ham.

December 20 Communication

Say what?

If I say "three yards," your first thought is probably football. If I said the same thing to your wife, her first thought would probably be cloth. Of course, the depth of male/female communication problems goes far beyond that cute example. You say something, and what your wife hears is very different. She says something, and what it means to you is nothing like what she intended to communicate. Some of it's a gender difference, but it's also a result of differences in personality, life experience, and how our brains work.

The big challenge is learning to know when we have not communicated. How may times have you been frustrated with your wife for not doing something you felt you clearly asked her to do? How many times has she been upset with you for not doing something when or how she thought you said you would do it? Perhaps most of these situations occurred because you didn't really understand each other. Become aware of these situations, and work to prevent problems by ensuring that you know exactly what she is saying, and she knows exactly what you are saying.

December 21 Walk

Forgive

Today's tip is unashamedly stolen from the Generous Wife – hey – when she's right, she's right!

Unforgiveness is a heavy burden, especially when it's with your wife. Pray for God to show you any unforgiveness you have toward your wife so that you can deal with it. Also, pray about anything she needs to forgive you for, and how you can help her to do that.

"And whenever you stand praying, forgive ..." (Mark 11:25)

December 22 Holiday/Words

Show her off a bit.

Do you have time with extended family coming up for the holidays? Praising your wife in front of her family, or yours, is about the best, most meaningful praise she will ever receive. Make sure everyone knows that you love her, admire her, adore her, and feel extremely blessed to have her as your wife.

Hint: Patting her on the butt in front of her mother is not usually considered a good way of accomplishing the above!

➢➢ **Have I mentioned that she's worth it?** ➣➣

December 23 Gifts

Time to Stockpile!

If your wife is into chocolate (and most are) this is the time of the year to stock up. Find a really good place to hide the stash, and then dole it out over the next couple of months. The less obviously Christmas candies are best, but a true chocoholic is not going to care that her January fix is in the form of a toy soldier or a snowman.

December 24 Holiday/Time

Not a creature stirring...

After everyone else is in bed (or you have banished older kids to their rooms) sit together with your wife in front of the Christmas tree or a lit candle, and share your thoughts. Talk about what your faith means to you. Talk about your dreams. Hold her close and let her soak it up for a long time.

December 25 Holiday/Time

What a gift she is.

Find a moment of privacy today, even if you have to drag her into the garage, and tell her that after salvation, she's the most precious gift you've ever received. Give her a long hug, and wish her a Merry Christmas.

Hints: If you have kids, take advantage of the have-to-try-every-toy-now aspect of Christmas. If you're away from home, take a short walk in the afternoon or evening.

December 26 Service

The Day After

Chances are there's post festivities mess at your house. Do something to help your wife – clean, keep the kids busy, or take everyone out to eat so she doesn't have to cook again.

If you really love her, offer to do the gift exchanges/returns or go out for batteries and/or adapters that you lack.

December 27 Touch

...till she drops.

Does your wife do the after-Christmas-shopping-till-she-can't-move-any-more thing? Be ready with a foot and leg massage.

➢➢ *"He who finds a wife finds a good thing."* Pr 18:22b⋖⋖

December 28 Words

Did you notice?

Has she been working over-time to get ready for Christmas? Have you seen the extra cleaning, the decorating, the wrapping, and the cooking? A few words of thanks and encouragement right about now will be a well-received blessing.

December 29 Walk

Split the work, but get all the blessings.

Get a thru the Bible in a year program, and "split the work." One of you reads the OT entry each day; the other reads the NT entry. Then tell each other what you've read.

December 30 Words

The Year in Review

Think about the last year, and come up with some "highlights" which show your wife doing a great job; then share these things with your wife. Mention things that demonstrate a deepening commitment to the Lord, growth, or achievement. Don't forget to talk about things that come under the category of her being a generous wife.

December 31 Time

Next year...

Make a commitment to spend more time with your wife next year than you did this last year. Don't just make an internal commitment, make a verbal promise to her, and to God, that you will find ways to spend more time with her no matter what it costs. (Note: If you are in the .2% of men who spend enough time with their wife, you may ignore this.)

Hot Bonus: If you're going to be home at midnight, try ringing in the New Year with sex. Grab her at the appropriate time and tell her you want to make love to her for the rest of the year!

The Most Difficult and Costly Gift

You can't buy it any store, and it costs no money, but it will cost you far more than anything else you can give: being a loving, godly, generous husband. It means picking up the socks you always leave 6 inches from the hamper even though you know she would do it and not complain. It means going more often to the restaurant she really likes that you don't much care for. It means giving her your time even when you're tired, busy, or grumpy. It means sacrificing for her, giving to her, and putting her first in every way. It may mean being willing to "look silly," doing things you don't want to do, or giving up some thing you hold dear. It's not easy, and it takes a "real man" to make it happen.

Few men even try – will you?

Buying Lingerie Without Dying of Embarrassment

So, you'd like to buy her some sexy underwear, but haven't a clue about how to do it? If you go armed with a bit of information about lingerie, and how it's sized, you just might escape without your face becoming brighter red than the panties you are buying.

First tip: don't start at the big name lingerie stores at the mall; these will both embarrass you, and assault your wallet. Wal*Mart®, Target®, and other "discount stores" have very nice looking items, better prices, and a less intimidating atmosphere.

First – do no harm (don't offend her).

In addition to not embarrassing yourself, you don't want to offend your wife. What you buy for her is making a statement about how you view her sexuality; if that statement clashes significantly with how she sees herself, trouble may result. You want her reaction to be, "He must think I'm hot" not, "He must think I'm a slut."

Consider what she wears now; it's a statement about how she sees her sexuality. If you've never given her lingerie before, start with something only slightly racier than what she currently wears. If she only wears white and pastels, something black with red trim is over the top. If all she owns are "granny panties," a bikini (not a string bikini) may seem pretty sexual to her. On the other hand, if she has thongs and open cup bras, you probably can't shock or offend her.

If you need to go low-key, try solid dark colours like blue, green, or purple. Solid black or red are much more sexual; if she may be nervous about such items, avoid them - or put one in with some tamer things. A black background with flowers on it is a good "compromise."

If you want to try something that you think she will find "adventurous," give the special item along with other less wild things. Tell her that the adventurous item is "a gift for me."

Very important: If she doesn't already own a thong, don't buy her one!

Size, size, what is her size?

Lingerie sizes are really a sick joke – so go armed with some measurements, getting her size off items she's comfortable in. You want waist size, dress size, T-shirt size, and bra size (the number is her chest under her breasts; the letter/cup size is how much bigger she is measured around at the nipples).

Bras are easy to size, but then you have other options. Again, let her current attire guide you: If none of her bras has an under-wire (a stiff insert under each cup), don't buy a bra that does. If she does not own a push up bra, don't get her one. If all of her bras have a bit of padding, buy the same, unless it going to be bedroom-wear only (padding reduces nipple show through). Unless she does not own a single back-hook bra, don't worry about front vs. back closure. Hint: a front closure is easier and more fun for you!

The size on panties has no correlation to pant size, or dress size, or any other aspect of reality. To make it more confusing, the size numbers (or letters) vary from one manufacturer to another – so a size 7 from the one lingerie company may be much smaller than a size 7 from another company.

Your best bet is to check a pair of her panties and "measure" them. Get a pair of panties that are not too old and thus stretched out. Put one side of the waistband on your extended pointer finger, and gently pull them along your arm, noting how far they go with moderate force. Repeat at the store, **when you are absolutely sure no one is watching**! Otherwise, check the size on her panties at home, and try to find the same brand at the store. If you have her actual waist size, a clerk can help – if you're willing to ask!

Some items, especially looser things like teddies, are small, medium, large, and maybe extra large. You can probably guess fairly well at this – go by T-shirt size. When in doubt, get a bigger size.

OS stands for "one size fits all." **DO NOT BELIEVE IT.** If your wife is over 30 or has ever had a baby, forget about OS.

Daywear vs. Playwear

Some women have two kinds of lingerie – what they wear under their clothes, and what they wear in private for their husband. Some items are not practical or comfortable for extended wear, and those items we most like to see them in tend to fit in this category. Let your wife know that her comfort is important to you, and that you are fine with her putting certain items on just so you can take them off.

Non-Sexual Massage

(Sexual massage on page 208)

Non-sexual massage is great for a woman who has a difficult time dealing with sex; it's also good any time a woman needs some non-sexual touch. Strictly non-sexual massage is particularly important for a woman with sexual abuse in her past, and it can be helpful for many women who struggle with sex.

Touch is important for all of us and it affects our bodies and minds in profound ways (see information on oxytocin on page 158). The same attitudes, fears, and damage that make sex difficult also cut a woman off from receiving needed touch. The following massage is designed to be as non-sexual and non-threatening as possible.

In order for massage to work for a woman who has trouble with sex, it must be TOTALLY NON-SEXUAL!! It may take a while for her to relax and believe it's not just "a trick just to get sex," but perseverance should win out. The "rules" for non-sexual massage:

- A whole body massage is just for her.
- Make it clear that your only intention is to bless her. You don't want, nor will you ever be willing to receive, anything in return.
- Massage is NEVER, EVER TO BE FOLLOWED BY SEX. Set a minimum 2 hour "no sex" limit following the massage.
- You need to wear something to cover your genitals; you will get aroused, but this should not be "advertised."

To start, have her shower. Better yet, give her a long hot bubble bath – prepare it for her, and leave her alone to soak. While she is in the bath, prepare you massage space. The bed isn't a good place to give a massage; aside from possible sexual connotations, it's not firm enough. Make a place for the massage on the floor; fold a blanket to give comfort, and cover with towels to protect the blanket. If you have good think carpet, a beach towel may be all you need. You will need a good deal of room; make sure you can move freely around where your wife will be laying. The room needs to be warm enough to prevent her from feeling cool; this means it's going to be too warm for you. Have ready several pillows, towels to cover the pillows, and massage oil kept warm by floating in a container of hot water. See page 173 for homemade massage oil.

When she's clean and dry, have her lay face down on the space you've prepared. Place a small pillow for her head, and another under her legs just above the feet. Apply the oil to your hands, not directly to her skin. Start with her shoulders and work down, slowly. Learn where she carries tension and pay special attention to those areas; the shoulders and neck are common tension spots. Your strokes should be toward her heart, or use firm strokes moving toward her heart followed by lighter return strokes. Avoid pressing on her spine as you move down her back. When you reach her feet, turn her over, and work back up to the head. Avoid her genitals. A brief, light massage of her breasts may be okay in the future, but avoid this initially. Finish with her face.

The hands and feet are especially important, spend extra time on them, but be careful with the feet as they are easily tickled. Use a firm touch to avoid tickling but be careful - too much pressure in the wrong place can cause pain. Remember, relaxation is the primary goal. A good thorough massage should take at least 30 minutes. Say very little as you work; let her concentrate on this "safe" touch that she can enjoy. When you finish, lie next to her and snuggle (be sure not to "poke" her if you're aroused). Speak softly and tell her you love her. Just let her relax and enjoy.

Non-sexual massage really helped Lori and me. It gave her the touch she needed in a safe way she could receive. It demonstrated my sacrificial love to her; she knew how turned on I got, but I never pursued it. It taught her that not all men were molesters (she knew it, but this got it into her heart), and it taught her how to receive and enjoy touch. I learned how to give without seeking anything in return, and how to put my wife's needs first in a practical way.

Try giving your wife a "whole body rub." Try doing it often. Do it when she is tired, tense, overwhelmed, grumpy, and so on. In addition, try doing it every time you're mad at her!

Cooking for Those Who Are "Clueless About the Citchen."

Presentation is everything when it comes to a "fine dining" experience. Candles, good plates, and cloth napkins make whatever you fix seem better. Another thing that makes it nice is making sure she doesn't have to do anything; **don't forget to clean up!**

If You Really Shouldn't Cook

If you really shouldn't cook, or just don't have time, you can fake it very nicely with heat-and-eat items by transferring them to serving dishes and plates.

Frozen lasagna is a great "cheat meal." Be aware that it's likely to take longer to heat than the box says; check the center to see if it's hot enough. Add heat-and-eat bread sticks or rolls and a fancy frozen vegetable complete with sauce. Buy a "salad kit" in a bag and add a tomato and a few olives.

For dessert, you can't go wrong with cheesecake. Buy fresh made in the bakery section, or frozen (be sure to thaw it well). If you buy plain cheesecake, stop by the baking aisle for canned pie fillings. Refrigerate the filling and spread on the top of the cheesecake before serving.

If You Want to Brave It

Even if you don't know a pot from a kettle, you can make a decent meal with a bit of instruction. Below are recipes ranging from embarrassingly easy to rather fancy. Please note that as written, these recipes do not result in kitchen fires or food poisoning.

Recipes from the Generous Kitchen

Pg #	Recipe
192	**Chicken Tortilla Soup** A meal all by it's self
192	**Blue Cheese Rolls** Very fancy, very easy
193	**Fresh Asparagus** It's not that hard, really
193	**Hollandaise Sauce** The ultimate in elegance
194	**Swedish Meatballs** A do ahead crock pot meal
194	**Honey Lemon Fruit Salad** Light and tasty – salad or dessert
195	**Beef Stroganoff** A manly dish that she'll like too
195	**Cheese Sauce** Covers a multitude of (cooking) sins
196	**Easy Fruit Cobbler** Easy, but incredible
196	**Magic Toast** Must try to understand

Recipes from the Generous Bedroom!

197	**Chocolate Flavoured Edible Body Power** Makes you lickable
197	**Honey Dust** Be sure to get every last bit
197	**Chocolate Body Paint** Sex is no longer low cal

Chicken Tortilla Soup

Soup Ingredients:
4 chicken breasts, cooked (boiled) and cubed
1 10 oz can diced tomatoes with green chilies
2 15 oz cans tomato sauce
6 cans water (use a tomato sauce can)
6 cubes chicken bouillon
½ a medium onion, chopped
salt and garlic (or garlic salt) to taste

Other Ingredients:
avocados, sliced
cheese, shredded
sour cream
black olives, sliced
tortilla chips, broken

Mix all soup ingredients in a large pot and heat to boiling. Simmer 15 minutes to an hour.

To serve: Place broken chips in the bottom of bowl, then ladle on soup. Garnish with other items, cheese and sour cream first.

Blue Cheese Dinner Rolls

Buy brown and serve dinner rolls (probably refrigerated at the grocery) and some crumbled blue cheese. Use a spoon and a small bowl to mix the blue cheese with an equal amount of softened butter. Follow directions on the rolls, but before putting them in the oven pull each one open and put in a teaspoon of the butter and blue cheese mix.

Fresh Asparagus

Buy fresh asparagus - a pound is plenty for two adults. Tie (with light twine) bundles of 10 to 12 stocks, and place them upright or slightly leaning in a tall pot. You want the tips out of the 3 inches of water you add to the pot. Bring to a boil and then cover (use a foil tent if the pot is too short). Cook for 8 minutes.
Try to time so the asparagus is done when it's time to sit down. Remove, from pot, cut string, and place in a serving dish. Add a generous amount of butter.

Hollandaise Sauce

(serve over eggs, fish or vegetables)

1 1/3 cup butter
4 large egg yokes
3 Tbs lemon juice
1/8 tsp salt
dash (less than 1/8 tsp) cayenne or hot pepper sauce
5 Tbs hot water (boiled then remove from heat)

Heat butter in sauce pan until hot and foamy, but not browned.
In a small bowl, whisk egg yokes with lemon juice, salt, and cayenne pepper or hot sauce. Gradually beat in butter, then water.
Return mixture to sauce pot and beat over very low heat until slightly thickened.
Serve immediately, or let stand over hot water for up to thirty minutes.

Swedish Meatballs

1 lb frozen meatballs
1 can cream of mushroom soup
2 Tbs melted butter
1/3 cup water
½ cup sour cream
2 beef bouillon cubes
1/3 cup milk
1/8 tsp salt
1/8 tsp pepper

In a large bowl combine all ingredients except meat balls and bouillon. Wisk until combined and all lumps are removed.

Transfer to a pot, add bouillon, and heat to simmer, stirring occasionally.

Place meatballs in crock pot, pour sauce over meat balls. Cover and cook on high for 3 hours, and low for one more hour. Serve over noodles or rice.

Honey Lemon Fruit Salad

1 small apple, chopped
1 cup seedless grapes, cut lengthwise
1 (11 oz.) can mandarin orange slices, drained
2 Tbs lemon juice
2 Tbs honey
¼ tsp cinnamon

Mix honey, lemon, and cinnamon together.
Mix fruit. Pour sauce over fruit. Refrigerate covered.

Beef Stroganoff

1 lb ground beef
1 small onion, chopped
4 beef bouillon cubes
2/3 cup sour cream
2 tsp flour
1 cup water
1 cup mushrooms (fresh or canned)
½ tsp minced garlic
½ tsp salt
¼ tsp pepper

Brown meat, onion, and garlic in skillet; drain off fat. Stir in water, mushrooms, bouillon, salt, and pepper. Cook over medium heat until heated through and mushrooms are tender.
Combine sour cream and flour. Stir into skillet and heat until sauce is thickened, about 5 minutes. Do not boil. Serve over noodles.

Cheese Sauce
(serve over broccoli)

1/4 cup. butter
1/4 cup. flour
2 cup. milk, warm
1 tsp. salt
1/4 tsp. pepper
1 cup shredded cheddar

Melt butter in saucepan. Stir in flour. Add milk and cook until slightly thick. Add cheese, salt, pepper and cheese.

Easy Fruit Cobbler

4 cups of fruit (peaches, pears, apples or berries)
½ cup white sugar
2 Tbs Bisquick
1 tsp cinnamon
1 1/3 cup Bisquick
1 cup Brown Sugar
½ cup cold butter (1 stick)

Preheat oven to 400° F.
In a bowl combine the fruit, white sugar, and 2 Tbs of Bisquick. Stir until well mixed. Pour into greased 8x8 inch backing pan.
In dry bowl, combine brown sugar and remaining Bisquick, and mix well. Spread mixture evenly over the top of fruit mixture.
Cut butter length wise, then cut halves lengthwise, giving 4 long pieces. Cut into cubes and dot evenly over Bisquick mixture.

Bake for 25 to 35 minutes. Remove when toping is well browned.

Magic Toast

Generously butter slices of bread. Sprinkle cinnamon on top of butter, and then add enough brown sugar to cover all of the butter. Transfer to toaster oven – use broiler setting for a soft bottom, or toaster setting for a dry toasty bottom. Heat until sugar is bubbly, watch for burning. Remove with spatula and allow to cool slightly – it will burn skin!

Chocolate Flavoured Edible Body Power

3 parts cornstarch
1 part powdered sugar
1 part cocoa powder

Sift ingredients together, and put in a shaker bottle.

Honey Dust

1Tbl of vanilla powder (specialty item, look on-line)
1 cup of cornstarch
1Tbl pure honey

Mix dry ingredients, then add honey. Work honey into the powder, rubbing clumps between hands to reduce it to very tiny particles. Apply with a feather or large brush.

Chocolate Body Paint

6 ounces fine-quality bittersweet chocolate
½ cup heavy cream
1 Tbl white granular sugar

Chop chocolate into small pieces and place in bowl.
In a small saucepan, bring cream and sugar just to a simmer, stirring until sugar is dissolved. Pour liquid over chocolate. Stir until chocolate is completely melted.
Sauce may be kept, chilled in an airtight container, for one week. Reheat sauce in a metal bowl, stirring occasionally, over a saucepan of simmering water. Check temperature before applying to body!

Extra Tips for Those Who Have Children at Home

By Proxy:

Obviously you should learn what each of your children's love language is, and give to them accordingly. Less obvious, be sure to give to your children in your wife's love language. Doing this blesses your wife because it makes her feel you are loving the children as you should. Use the following ideas as a starting place for giving to your children in the various areas discussed in this book.

Quality Time

Mothers care deeply for their kids, and especially for their emotional well-being. Because of this, spending time with your children is a blessing to your wife.

Time with your children need not be a big deal or involve a lot of planning; really, they just need to be with you. When our son was 2 and 3 years old, I was working many hours in the Texas heat. I was often too exhausted to do much with him in the evening, so I would simply lay on the floor and let him climb all over me. A few tickles and rolling him over now and then made it a great fun time with dad.

Bonus: Arrange some of your time with your child/children so that it gives your wife a break. This is good for your wife, your kids, and your marriage.

Prayer/Walk

Don't just teach your kids to pray, make sure they hear you pray. Likewise, live your faith in front of your children. Words are of little value, kids will do what you do, not what you say. Your wife may spend more time with them, and may discuss spiritual matters with them more, but knowing that dad is sold out for the Lord is vital.

Gifts

It blesses a mother's heart to see her husband bless his kids; so buying them gifts is almost like buying a gift for your wife. If you have a daughter, buying her flowers may bring tears to your wife's eyes. Boy gifts are less likely to open the floodgates, but they will still bless her.

You don't have to have a reason to give a small gift to your children, just do it because you love them. Teach them that gifts are given out of love, not to coax or reward certain behaviour. Keep your eyes open for items that fit your children's individual interests.

Words of Affirmation

Watch what you say! Hold back the unnecessary and unloving criticism, and look for ways to encourage your children frequently. Children are very sensitive to our words, and to the messages behind our words; they readily recognize anger, frustration, and disappointment be it in our words, our tone, or our body language. It's all too easy to damage the spirit of a child with a few careless words. On the other hand, you can deeply bless a child with well-timed encouragement, and can change their life forever with ongoing praise and affirmation.

If your wife is an encouraging words type person, she is especially sensitive to what you say to your children, both the positive and the negative. This sensitivity can lead to arguments about how you speak to the children. Because she's probably more in touch with the children, the odds are she's right about these matters. Any concerns your wife expresses along these lines deserve a great deal of thought and prayer.

Touch

Children have a massive need for touch. We tend to touch small children without even thinking about it, but as they grow up we may fail to keep giving them the touch they need.

Your son may not want to be hugged and kissed as he gets older, but he will accept a bit of wrestling or other "manly" contact. When and where you touch him, and especially who's watching, are also factors. Think back to when you were his age, and find ways to make contact that won't be rejected.

As your daughter becomes a young woman, you may be unsure how to touch her - **do not allow this stop you!** How you touch a 6 year old differs from how you touch a 16 year old, but the need for her daddy's touch does not end at puberty. Girls who don't receive touch from their fathers are much more likely to seek out touch from boys their age – and you know what kind of touch they want! One good form of touch for a daughter is a shoulder rub. Start when she's young, and continue as she grows up.

Acts of Service

Acts of service for children are often a trial – from being a "horsie" to building a tree house. What they want of you can be maddeningly boring, maddeningly silly, or just plain maddening. It's also very important.

It's easy to put off our kid's needs because they seem so trivial to us, but they're not trivial to them. Long after they forget what you did for them, they will remember that you did things for them, and that you were there for them. Helping them with what is important to them is what blesses them; and it blesses your wife as well.

Communication

Granted, you're not going to have a deep conversation with a 3 year old; the same is true for most 13 year olds. If you want to be able to talk with your children when they are old enough "for it to matter," you will have to build lines of communication early, and keep those lines open as they grow.

Young children have very short attention spans, and trying to keep them on one subject too long is only going to frustrate both of you. Go with their flow, and express interested in what they want to "discuss."

Grade school children seem to have sudden bursts of intellectual maturity surrounded by long periods during which it's clear nobody's home. The only way to catch enough of the brilliant periods to matter is to spend regular time talking with them.

Teens have the annoying habit of not hearing what is said to them, even when they really heard. It's not you; this is how they deal with their uncertainty or embarrassment. Just keep talking; they hear you even when they don't show it.

Sex

In a world where sex is cheap, you can help your kids see sex as it should be by giving them a good example. Obviously, you don't let them see you having sex, but you can demonstrate that you and your wife both desire and enjoy each other. By showing them that sex in marriage is good, you give them a reason to wait. That little pat on mom's butt may bring a round of protests, but the message it sends is more powerful than any lecture you could give.

Other Things:

If you have kids at home, making private time with your wife can be challenging. A few ideas:

Send Them Away and Stay Home

Try to get them out of the house with a "baby sitter" on Saturday. Send them to the park, the pool, a movie, or some other age-appropriate place. If you put your funds into "child care" and stay home with your wife it can be a relatively "cheap date." Rent a couple of movies, play games you used to play, or chase each other around naked.

You Keep Mine, I'll Keep Yours

Find a couple with kids the same general age as yours, and switch off; you get them all, then they get them all. This works for an evening or a weekend.

College Nanny

College age young adults are always looking for a few extra dollars. Find a responsible individual – the offspring of a family friend or someone at your church – who would be willing to spend a few days playing nanny. Set the nanny up in your guest room and provide easy to fix meals.

This idea works very well during the school week if you can find someone who can be home during the time the kids are not in school. If you can swing the days off, weekday vacationing is a great way to go.

Family Time

Be sure to have family time that includes you, your wife, and your children. They need it, your wife needs it, and truth be told you need it too. Play a game, read a book aloud, go for walks, have family devotionals, eat as a family both out and at home.

Will that be with or without children?

I've heard women complain that their husband wants to, "include the kids in everything," and I've heard other wives complain that their husband "never includes the children." This occurs even when the two families have the same amount of "family time."

Some women seem to have little need for time without the children; others go crazy if they don't get time without the kids. There's no right or wrong here, only what your wife needs. Find out how she feels, and make it a significant factor in your planning.

The Flood, AKA Menstruation

NOTE: If your wife is post-menopausal, pregnant, or using hormonal contraceptives, the following does not apply.

A woman's menstrual cycle affects virtually every aspect of her life, including her sexuality. It would be difficult to overstate the impact her cycle has on her. Knowing where she is in her cycle can make life easier for both of you; it can also make sex a lot better for both of you. Her cycle affects her mood, her energy level, how she reacts to things, and much more. One study even showed that the "time of the month" affects a woman's ability to do math calculations!

We guys have one sex hormone; our wives have several. Our hormone cycles once a day, theirs ebb and flow over 28 days, give or take. In addition to each of her hormones changing daily, the individual hormones interact, and affect the levels of many other hormones. In short, your hormone is a single drum, while her hormones are a full orchestra.

My goal here is to give you the ability to track her cycle, and an understanding of how she is likely to change throughout her cycle. With this information, you can make notes about her mood, her sex drive, or whatever else, and learn to be ready for what her hormones throw at you.

Traditionally a woman's cycle is counted with the first day of bleeding as "day one." This is easy, but it's not overly useful because this day is not a hormonal starting place. If her cycle is very regular, using the beginning of her period as day one will work fairly well, but if her cycles vary, this starting place will not really help you track her moods and desires. The reason for this complexity is that the number of days from ovulation (release of an egg) to menstruation (bleeding) is consistent for all of her cycles – 14 days for most women, a bit more or less for a few. If her cycles vary, the extra days are between the first day of her period and when she ovulates. Ovulation is the hormonal starting place – but you can't know when ovulation occurs until menstruation starts 14 days later. Leave it to a woman to be so mysterious!

There is a way to work around this unknown. If you keep track of her moods and desires on a calendar, then add her cycle after you know it, you will soon see patterns emerge. You will likely see that she is sexually aggressive a day before she ovulates, or that she strongly resists sex for the three days after she ovulates, or that she is giddy on such and such day, or distant on certain days, or tired, or easily upset with the kids, and so on. Once you put these things into context with her cycle, they will become signposts you can use to estimate where she is in her cycle even before her period gives you confirmation. Learn to read the hints, and you can know what is coming next.

Enough explanation, let's start tracking. Get a date book or notebook for keeping your records. Start making daily notes about the things you want to track; her mood, energy level, sex drive, complaints and frustrations are all good things to watch.

When she starts her period, count back two weeks and make that day zero. So, if she starts her period on a Wednesday, she ovulated two weeks earlier, also on a Wednesday. Once you have the "zero day" fill in positive numbers forward, which makes the day she starts to menstruate day 14. Next, put in negative numbers from zero back to the start of her last period. After you have a few cycles you can start to look for certain moods or events that occur on the same or nearly the same numbered day. You may be shocked at what you learn; things that have always seems random suddenly have a predictable pattern!

Use your newfound insight to bless your wife and to make life easier for both of you. Don't invite guests over when she will be tired or grumpy, help with the kids when she's going to have a hard time coping, plan your activities and dates with her mood and energy in mind, and make the most of the times when she is more interested in, and most able to enjoy sex.

Sexual Patterns

Her cycle affects her sexuality in many ways, some of them rather extreme. Figure out the "code" and you will be able to make sex much better for both of you. Because every woman is somewhat different, you will need to study your wife to learn how her hormones affect her sexuality. Getting a handle on it can be well worth your while. Below are a few common patterns, as a starting place:

- Most women have their strongest sex drive just before they ovulate, building for a few days and peaking on the day before or the day of ovulation.

- Many women have a "receptive sex drive" prior to the above – she won't chase you, but may enjoy being chased.
- Following ovulation, drive drops significantly and rapidly.
- There may be a "rebound" in desire shortly before her period.
- The type and duration of stimulation she wants/needs during foreplay can vary greatly during the month. The same thing is true for intercourse.
- There may be certain days (probably the week before ovulation) when it's easier for her to climax during intercourse, and other days (probably the week after ovulation) when it's difficult or essentially impossible for her to do so.
- She may want or be able to have multiple orgasms only during a certain part of the month.
- There may be a part of the month where it takes longer to reach climax, but the result is more earth shattering.
- She may be interested in receiving, or giving, certain kinds of stimulation at one time of the month, but not at other times.

Many women are not aware, or not fully aware, of the way their cycle affects their sexuality. It may be that it's difficult to see it from "in there." However, from "out here" it's fairly obvious once you know what to look for. Learn to know where she is in her cycle, and keep that in mind as you have sex with her.

Sexual Massage

If you skipped the non-sexual massage section on page 187, go back, and read it – this section builds on that one.

Massage is inherently sexual, and you easily can make it very sexual. If a woman enjoys sex, a massage from her husband will touch her sexual side. Unless you so relax her that she's almost asleep, there's a good chance your efforts will arouse her; in addition to the intimacy of massage, your touch releases a great deal of oxytocin into her body, and that tends to be arousing. If she's open to it, massage can be a great form of foreplay, first relaxing her, and then arousing her. If you get it just right, you won't be allowed to finish the massage!

To start, have her take a shower. Consider getting in the shower with her and doing the washing for her. When she's dry (do that for her too) have her lay face down. Start at her feet, and work up, slowly. Feet can be ticklish, so be careful – firm pressure will reduce tickling. Your strokes should be toward her heart, or use firm strokes moving toward her heart and soft return strokes. Spend extra time on her rear end, as it's a sensual area. You can use your full hands and a good deal of pressure on her rear. Avoid pressing on her spine as you move up her back. Learn where she carries tension, and pay special attention to those areas; the shoulders and neck are common tension spots. Massaging her back side is mostly to relax her. Get the tension and the cares of the day out of the way so you can arouse her.

When you reach her head, turn her over, and start the arousing side of the massage. The face is a sensuous area for a woman, so spend a bit of time there; use light fingertip massage tracing her features.

Work down the front of her arms and do her hands before you move to her breasts. Don't just grab her breasts; tease her. Move your hands over her breasts gently, then move around to the outside edge, and back around to the top. Cup as you rub, using one hand on each breast or both hands on one breast. Give some special attention to the nipples, but only after you have spent plenty of time on the rest of the breast. Don't squeeze the nipple too firmly or twist it too hard.

Work on downward now, but don't be in a hurry to get to her genitals. Anticipation is a good thing; make her really want you to get there. Move over and around her tummy, and then run your hands down the outside of her legs. Bring your hands in and come back up the inside of the legs. Follow the line where her leg and groin meet, just barely caressing the far edge of her vulva as you go by. Do this several times before you focus on her genitals. You want her legs apart now – lift and bend at the knee, then rotate the leg outward to give good access to her vulva. A pillow under each knee will make her more comfortable. Vary soft strokes with firm ones, fingertips with the whole palm. Upward strokes are usually to be more stimulating than downward ones. Be careful not to over stimulate her.

From here you're on your own; play it by ear. You can finish the massage back down to her feet, massage her genitals until she orgasms, or move to some other sex act. Intercourse with a "well oiled" wife is a different experience for both.

A note on oil for sexual massage: If you are going to be touching her genitals with the oil, you want to be careful about adding scents. Any kind of mint can produce a burning sensation if it's too strong, so avoid them unless you know you will not be hitting her most sensitive places. Oil on the vulva is fine. A small amount of oil in the vagina is not usually a problem, but don't get anything scented inside of her. Be aware that oil can interfere with condoms and spermicides.

Suggested Reading List

This list is short for two reasons; you probably don't have a lot of time, and I only recommend books that I think have the potential to make a real difference in your life.

The Five Love Languages by Gary Chapman

A must read. Learn how your wife hears love so you can give to her in that area of her life.

Gentlemen, Start Her Engine by Steven A. Guerrero

A unique tool that will help you understand your wife so you can customize how you romance her. This book could be sub-titled "How to win her heart for dummies." Order from the author's web site at www.startherheart.com.

Sheet Music by Dr. Kevin Leman

I think this is by far the best "Christian sex book" on the market. Truth both Biblical and biological is brought together with humour that will have you laughing out loud. Whether you have sexual problems or just want to improve a good thing, this is the book to help you.

Wild at Heart by John Elderedge

More than just a book, this is a way of life. *Wild at Heart* is about "recapturing masculinity" so a man can be the husband and father God intended him to be. The author deals with early wounding that keeps men from being what they should be, and causes them to be what they don't want to be.

Intimate Issues by Linda Dillow and Lorraine Pintus

An outstanding book about sex that is written for and by women. This book has been given credit by both men and women for major changes in how women think, feel, and engage in sex. If your wife is having trouble being sexual, this is the book for her.

Loving Solutions by Gary Chapman

If your wife is "truly difficult," you desperately need this book. The author shares practical insight into dealing with a variety of serious marital problems. At the very least, this book will help you better understand your situation, and it might give you ideas that will help bring about a change.

The Power of a Praying Husband by Stormie Omartian

If you don't know how to pray for your wife, here's the help you need. Written by a woman, it gets to the heart of what a woman needs.

New King James Version of the Bible

It's been said that the best version of the Bible is the one you read - no argument from me on that. However, if you are looking for a new Bible I highly recommend the NKJV. The language reads like modern English, and the integrity of the translation is excellent.

The Song of Songs by Ariel and Chana Bloch

If you want to study and understand the most sexual and misunderstood book of the Bible, this is an excellent text. You will never look at your Bible in quite the same way!

On-Line Resources

Be Broken Ministries:
http://www.bebroken.com/
An excellent ministry that helps men affected by pornography and sexual addiction. Also has resources for women married to these men. On-line individual help and programs designed for churches. Be Broken's book *Understanding Shame: Breaking the Power of the Addictive Spiral* is outstanding – you will find it in resources/books.

Book22:
http://www.book22.com/
A Christian, no nudity site offering intimacy enhancers for married couples. Vibrating eggs, body paint and powders, flavored condoms, and more shipped in plain boxes. No e-mail or snail mail advertising, and no sale of address lists.

My Davinci:
http://www.mydavinci.com/
You e-mail a photo, and they turn it into anything from a caricature to an oil painting. A great gift idea.

How Men Really Think about Sex:
www.christianitytoday.com/mp/2002/002/4.36.html
An outstanding article by Paula Rinehart, a female counselor. She explains what sex means to men very accurately, and in a way that makes sense to women.

The Generous Husband:
http:**//www.the-generous-husband.com/**

The web site that came before the book. You will find some resources not in the book, and a way to sign up for daily e-mail tips.

The Generous Wife:
http://www.the-generous-wife.com/
Trust me guys, you want my wife telling your wife how to be generous. Various resources and daily e-mail tips.

The Marriage Bed:
http://www.themarriagebed.com/
The web site that started it all. Articles designed to deal with sexual problems and enhance your sex life. Also an on-line discussion forum with close to 2000 members.

Marriage Counseling:
http://aacc.net
The American Association of Christian Counselors website. Click on "Find a Counselor."

About the Author

Born in Wyoming, Paul got to Texas as soon as he could, at the age of four. He's lived in Austin the last 39 years. Today Paul, his wife Lori, and their son live in his childhood home; the grown girl child lives across town.

Paul is the sole proprietor and only employee of Byerly Creations, a company that does a variety of things including landscaping, lawn maintenance, irrigation, fencing, and deck work.

Paul married Lori in 1985. Their otherwise good relationship was marred by sexual problems, problems for which the church was unable or unwilling to offer help. Years of struggling, reading, and praying followed, gradually resulting in victory.

In 1997 Paul and Lori began doing marriage ministry on the web, leading to the formation of The Marriage Bed, Inc., a non-profit, on-line ministry. "TMB" deals primarily with sexual issues of marriage, offering biblically sound and scientifically accurate information on intimacy and sexuality.

Raised Presbyterian, as an adult Paul moved to nondenominational churches. Frustrated with the lack of depth and intimacy they found in "traditional churches," Paul and Lori became a part of the "home church movement" in 1999. In home church they found the closeness and intimacy they desired, and they have been actively involved in various home groups ever since. In 2002 Paul was ordained by The American Evangelistic Association, the covering organization for TMB.

Printed in the United States
23776LVS00008B/4-18